Marc Chagall

Ingo F. Walther / Rainer Metzger

MARC CHAGALL
1887–1985

Painting as Poetry

Benedikt Taschen

**This book was printed on 100 % chlorine-free bleached
paper in accordance with the TCF standard.**

© 1993 Benedikt Taschen Verlag GmbH
Hohenzollernring 53, D-50672 Köln
© The reproductions: VG Bild-Kunst, Bonn, 1993
General editor: Ingo F. Walther, Alling
English translation: Michael Hulse, Cologne
Cover design: Angelika Muthesius, Cologne
Printed by Druckhaus Cramer GmbH, Greven

Printed in Germany
ISBN 3-8228-0567-X
GB

Contents

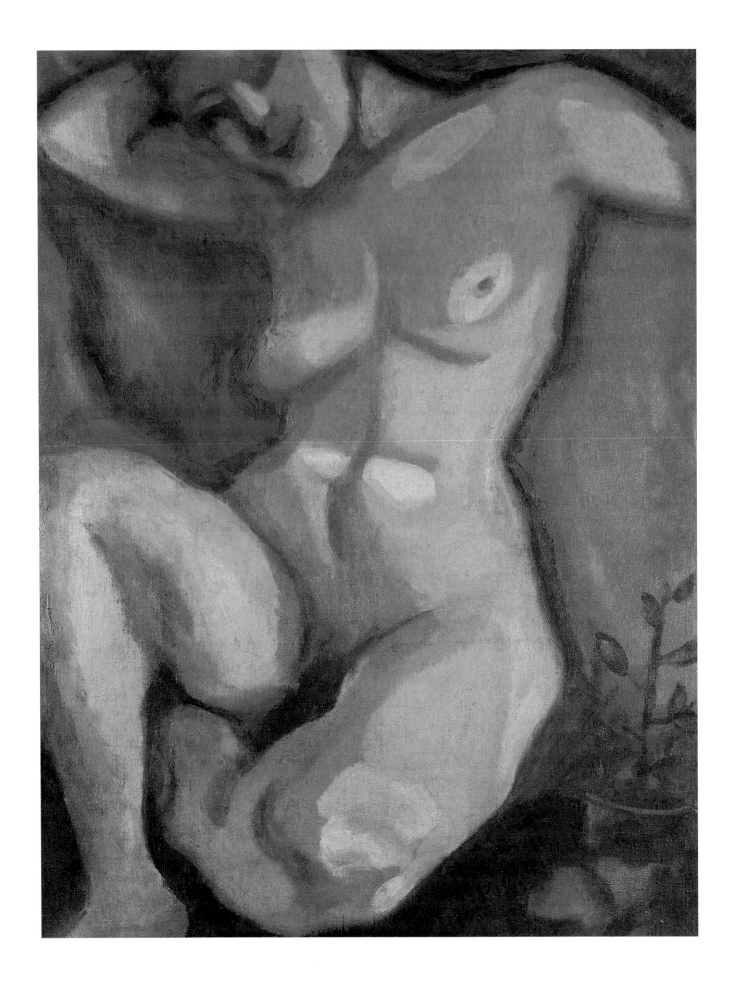

Russia: The Early Years 1887–1910

Marc Chagall: poet, dreamer, exotic apparition. Throughout his long life, the role of outsider and artistic eccentric came naturally to him. Chagall seemed a kind of intermediary between worlds: whether as a Jew with a lordly disdain for the ancient ban on image-making, or as a Russian who went beyond the realm of familiar self-sufficiency, or as the son of poor parents, growing up in a large and needy family, yet going on to establish himself in the sophisticated world of elegant artistic salons. The potential for assimilation and the liberality that distinguish Western culture are best assessed by its responses to outsiders; and Chagall personified the singular charm of the outsider his whole life long. His biography was far from everyday, and its reflection in his art took on the form of strange images. His life and art together added up to this image of a lonesome visionary, a citizen of the world with much of the child still in him, a stranger lost in wonder – an image which the artist did everything to cultivate. Profoundly religious and with a deep love of the homeland, his work is arguably the most urgent appeal for tolerance and respect of all that is different that modern times could make.

Marc Chagall, the eldest of nine children, was born on 7th July, 1887, into a family of Vitebsk Jews. The world of Eastern Jewry was both narrow and peaceful, going its quiet way between synagogue, fireside and shop (according to Chagall's own tongue-in-cheek account in *My Life*). Though only half of his home town's population of 50,000 were Jews, Vitebsk had all the characteristic traits of the *shtetl*: wooden houses, a rural atmosphere, poverty. Thanks to his mother, Marc was enabled to go on to the official state school after he had finished at the *cheder* (Jewish elementary school). Strictly speaking, Jews were not admitted to the state schools, but Feiga-Ita, enterprising woman that she was, bribed the teacher. So it was that Marc had the chance to escape the toils of neighbourly and nepotistic connections; instead of remaining trapped in humble confinement, he took violin and singing lessons, began to draw, and spoke Russian rather than Yiddish. Above all, he made contact with the

"My father had blue eyes but his hands were covered in calluses. He worked, prayed, and kept his peace. Like him, I was silent too. What was to become of me? Was I to stay like that my whole life long, sitting by a wall, or would I haul barrels about, too? I took a look at my hands. My hands were too soft . . . I had to find some special occupation, some kind of work that would not force me to turn away from the sky and the stars, that would allow me to discover the meaning of my life. Yes, that was what I was looking for. But in my home parts I was the only one who had ever uttered the words 'art' or 'artist'. 'What is an artist?' I asked." MARC CHAGALL

Red Nude Sitting Up, 1908
Oil on canvas, 90 × 70 cm
Private collection, London

**Young Girl on a Sofa
(Mariaska), 1907**
Oil on canvas, 72 × 92.5 cm
Private collection, Caracas

"With my 27 roubles in my pocket, the
only money my father ever gave me for a
journey, I disappear, still rosy-cheeked
and curly-haired, to St. Petersburg,
accompanied by my friends. The die is
cast."   MARC CHAGALL in *My Life*

bourgeois world where cosmopolitan and cultural interests were
valued; a life style that his father, Sachar, who sold herrings and
was perpetually weary, could never have offered him.

The young Chagall was persistent enough to obtain the
residence permit which Jews needed for the capital. In the winter
of 1906/1907, together with his friend Viktor Mekler, he moved to
St. Petersburg. In Vitebsk he had attended Yehuda Pen's art
school, and now he was out for a thorough artistic training in the
cultural heart of Russia. 'Young Girl on a Sofa' (above), a portrait
of his sister Mariaska, which he painted on a visit home in 1907, is
one of his earliest works and testifies to a new-found artistic
confidence (which was vital in view of his family's scepticism). As
if in a photograph, the girl is seen reclining on an outsize divan,
legs coquettishly crossed, wearing a beret. Chagall's family were
Orthodox Jews, but they were willing to be photographed, and so
this painting, with its everyday motifs and rather stiff pose, has

something of the familiar and accepted air of camerawork. The
decorative flatness, the blurred distinction between the figure
and the blanket and the soft, rounded lines contouring the body
reflect the influence of contemporary St. Petersburg painting.
None of this can quite conceal the technical weaknesses of the
piece, however, particularly evident in Mariaska's limbs.

The Family or Maternity, 1909
Oil on canvas, 74 × 67 cm
Private collection, New York

Russian Wedding, 1909
Oil on canvas, 68 × 97 cm
E. G. Bührle Collection, Zurich

The Village Street, 1909
Pencil and gouache on paper,
28.8 × 38 cm
Private collection, Paris

'Red Nude Sitting Up' (p. 6), painted a year later (also in Vitebsk), is a very different work, more powerful and of greater originality. Chagall had just won a scholarship to the celebrated Svanseva School where Léon Bakst taught, who was a major link with the West and an influential advocate of symbolist painting. Bakst wrote for the periodical *Mir Iskusstva (The World of Art)*. Through Bakst, Chagall acquired a finely tuned sense of his role as an artist and must have been helped towards new means of visual expression. In this new piece of work, the artist shows his nude frontally and with a weighty, direct physicality that is quite unlike the étude-like reticence of the picture of Mariaska. The unconventional red shades and their contrast with the green of the plant suggest that Chagall was familiar with recent French painting, in particular with that of Henri Matisse; an impression that is confirmed by the fragmented rendering of the figure, making it torso-like and rapt.

Chagall was not the smug and lordly artist-prince he portrayed himself as in the 'Self-portrait with Brushes' (p. 2), where we see him gazing disrespectfully out of the picture. But by 1909 he was no longer a naive lad either. Now, in his apprentice years in the capital, away from his own origins among the simple folk of the provinces, Chagall was able to turn to the subjects and motifs that were to be typical of his future work: village scenes, peasant life, intimate views of a small world. Not until he sensed this contrast with his Bohemian life in the big city, with its financial problems and the possibility of fame, did Chagall acquire his tender and loving eye for the life of the *shtetl*.

It is this tension that enriches the quality of another work of 1909, 'The Family or Maternity' (p. 9). The large areas, tranquil figures and simple gestures produce a monumental sense of dignity, translating everyday Jewish rituals into a timeless realm of iconic peacefulness. Compositionally, the painting derives from a traditional Western configuration of the circumcision of Christ with the high priest, madonna and child, with Joseph discreetly remaining in the background. Giving us the option of reading his painting allegorically by borrowing the formal arrangement of a Christian story for his everday scene, Chagall preserves the ambiguity of his own artistic technique, which was midway between naivety and symbolically gestural formality –

"My name is Marc, my emotional life is sensitive and my purse is empty, but they say I have talent."

MARC CHAGALL in *My Life*

Birth, 1910
Oil on canvas, 65 × 89.5 cm
Kunsthaus, Zurich

The Artist's Father, ca. 1907
Indian ink and sepia, 23 × 18 cm
Private collection, Moscow

"When I considered my father beneath his lamp I dreamt of skies and stars far from our street. All the poetry of life was in my father's sadness and silence, to my mind. There was the inexhaustible source of my dreams: my father, who could be compared to the immobile, secretive and silent cow that sleeps on the roof of the hut." MARC CHAGALL

Woman with a Bouquet, 1910
Oil on canvas, 64 × 53.5 cm
Helen Serger Collection, New York

much in the way that Paul Gauguin, his idol at that time, painted the Nativity in the South Seas.

'Russian Wedding' (p. 10), on the other hand, appears to be a genre painting, but in fact reflects a happy development in Chagall's own private life. In autumn 1909, through Thea Bachmann, he became acquainted with Bella Rosenfeld, the daughter of a Jewish jeweller, who also came from Vitebsk and who was studying in Moscow. She too had left her original homeland. In 1915 she was to marry Chagall, and many of his paintings, which were dedicated to her, were to draw their special harmony from their relationship.

In *My Life* Chagall writes that he "... found the house full of serious men and women," "and the crowds of black figures dimmed the daylight. Noise, whispers, then suddenly the piercing cry of a new-born child. Mama, half-naked, lay in bed, pale, a tender pink. My youngest brother was seeing the light of the world." In 1910 Chagall worked up this scene into the painting 'Birth' (p. 11), a key work in the art of his early Russian years. With its dramatic lighting, the scene might be happening on a stage, and shows what Chagall had learnt from Bakst, who often designed stage sets. To the left we see the exhausted mother lying on the bed, the sheets heavily bloodstained, the impact heightened by the red canopy. The wet-nurse, in hieratic posture, is holding the baby somewhat awkwardly. Beneath the bed crouches a bearded figure, maybe the father. From the right we see inquisitive neighbours and farmers shoving into the room (an old Jew is leading a cow) and others are participating in the happenings by looking in at the window.

The traditional cast of a Christian Nativity are all present here: the Holy Family, the wet-nurse and herdsmen, coming in to share in the event. But the artist has eliminated whatever the Biblical tale offers in the way of anecdote, and indeed there is a strict structural divison between the birth scene with the two women on the left, and the right-hand half where the men are mere onlookers. The personal experience described in *My Life,* the everyday event of birth, and the allusion to the Christian motif have all been integrated into a unifying structural principle that is fundamental and quite independent of any specific culture.

In 'Birth' we see at its most ambitious Chagall's attempt, so characteristic of his early work, and well documented in his autobiography, to transcend conceptual boundaries and create new syntheses. But even if the visual logistics are clear and assured, the formal solution remains unsatisfying. The ideas are persuasive, but the picture falls apart into two halves. In his quest for an artistic language that might render the complexity of his conceptual insights, Chagall could no longer expect inspiration from Russian art, itself in its infancy. The only place to find answers was in the capital of the art world: Paris.

The Paris Years
1910–1914

Russia's young up-and-coming artists were likelier to be better received in Paris than in their own country. Sergei Diaghilev's Russian Ballet, the entire troupe of dancers, musicians, writers and painters, had scored a sensation there with their mixture of sublimity and exoticism and had awakened longings for the vast spaces of the East. Russia was "in". Alexei von Jawlensky, Vassili Kandinsky, Jacques Lipchitz, and all the artists who were to achieve worldwide fame, took advantage of the fashion to get to know modernism at its place of birth. Bakst had arrived in 1909 to work with Diaghilev. In 1910 Chagall too made the four-day rail trip in the autumn, taking with him the spartan funds his St. Petersburg patron, Max Winawer, allowed him and hopes of being supported by the numerous Russians in Paris. He moved into his first studio on Montmartre, in a fellow Russian's flat.

"All that prevented me from returning immediately was the distance between Paris and my home town," Chagall writes in his memoirs, still complaining about the upheaval which so unsettled this country-born artist. Indeed, the young Chagall plunged into the world of art, going the rounds of galleries to see the Impressionists at Paul Durand-Ruel's, Gauguin and Vincent Van Gogh at the Galerie Bernheim (the first time he saw them in the original), and the astonishing Matisse at the autumn salon. Above all, he discovered the Old Masters: "The Louvre put an end to my uncertainty." In paintings such as 'The Model' (left), done soon after his arrival, we see his new engagement with the French artistic tradition. Chagall's palette, it is true, retains the earthy darkness of his Russian pictures, but the thick application of the paint and the frayed, fibrous juxtaposition of colourful brushstrokes reflect contemporary colour theories. Chagall's subject is a studio scene, and thus a meditation on his own work, but his model is holding a brush as well and painting a picture herself, which metaphorically creates an atmosphere of prevalent creativity, an artistic commitment that reaches into all aspects of everyday life. "Starting with the market, where I could only buy a

Self-portrait, 1910
Pen and black Indian ink on paper,
14.7 × 13.1 cm
Courtesy of the artist's family

The Model, 1910
Oil on canvas, 62 × 51.5 cm
Ida Chagall Collection

Self-portrait with Goat, 1922/23
Lithograph, 41 × 26.4 cm

" At that time I had grasped that I had to go to Paris. The soil that had nourished the roots of my art was Vitebsk; but my art needed Paris as much as a tree needs water. I had no other reason for leaving my homeland, and I believe that in my paintings I have always remained true to it. "   MARC CHAGALL

To My Betrothed, 1911
Gouache, oil and water-colour
on paper, 61 × 44.5 cm
Philadelphia Museum of Art,
Philadelphia

piece of a cucumber since I had no money; through the worker in his blue overalls, to the keenest disciples of Cubism, everything testified to a definite sense of measure and clarity, a precise sense of form, " writes Chagall, describing this creative flair. It was a flair he wanted to appropriate in his own work.

The artist did all that was in his power to promote the legend of his own poverty. Not only the cucumber he could only afford a piece of, not only the herring whose head he ate one day and tail the next, but even the very paintings he did in this early Paris period remind us of how poor Chagall was. Many of them are painted on canvas that had already been painted on and Chagall proved skillful at manipulating contrasts of light and dark, inherited through this re-use, for his own purposes of lighting. While the re-use of old canvases was good for demonstrating financial difficulties, in time it also became an expressive medium in its own right, and indeed a characteristic aesthetic procedure of the Cubists.

'Interior II' (p. 18), painted in 1911, shows us Chagall's first tentative ventures into Cubism. The Cubist idiom is seen in the angular shapes that mark the woman's skirt and the table edge, but beyond this seemingly abstract centre the picture also has a narrative content. In wild abandon, a woman is falling upon a bearded man and dragging a goat behind her. The man, who makes a fearful and defensive impression, cowering in his chair, is fending her off by grasping her thigh. The man's distress and the woman's wrathful instinctuality are conveyed by means of a centuries-old compositional trick by which, as in the reading process, we are made to interpret the dynamics of motion along a line from left to right.

In 'To my Betrothed' (right), painted at the same time, Chagall evolved a more contemporary approach to the same subject, though in the treatment of sexuality this painting is once again archetypal. Here, the full vitality of the subject is developed (albeit the compositional structure is distinguished by its total tranquillity within the terms of the visual medium): the woman twines about the shoulders of the bull-headed man like a snake, spitting into his face, while the man, with every appearance of calmness, grasps at her leg with a gesture that suggests desire rather than defence. The tale and its symbolic content are inseparable. They have become this way not only through the unity of human and animal, but particularly through the woman's radial movement, a demonstration of power which seems impossible for the man to escape from. If 'Interior II' could still be viewed as a harmless genre scene, that was no longer feasible now. Indeed, it was only after protracted argument that Chagall was allowed to exhibit this painting at the 1912 spring salon at all. He was accused of painting pornography. What gave this picture its bold suggestiveness was the simple compositional variation

of arranging the motifs in circular form about a centre rather than stringing them in one linear direction. It was a procedure Chagall had learnt from Cubism. In fact, Cubism was to solve many of Chagall's early technical problems.

Chagall's link with Cubism was forged not so much by Pablo Picasso or Georges Braque, the movement's founding fathers, as by Robert Delaunay, who was married to the Russian painter Sonia Terk. The orthodox Cubists' coolly dissecting gaze was not the way Chagall and Delaunay looked at things, nor were they interested in the solitary dignity of concrete objects, which enabled the Cubists to make even painted canvas their subject. And the dichotomy of abstraction and representation, Braque's and Picasso's integral method by which ordinary scrutiny of a thing would be amplified by everyday available knowledge of its uses, was of secondary importance to them too. For Delaunay, and especially for Chagall, Cubism represented an artistic language for the expression of the world's magic, the secret life of things, beyond mere functionality. It provided them with geometrical patterns, models for ordering dreams, experiences, desires and visions, ways of re-creating them in terms of a visual logic that could be grasped by others. Imagined realities were complicated enough, and needed an appropriate medium; and the Russian's visions, jostling for expression in his Paris years, found their needs answered to by the complexity of Cubist forms.

Near the Paris abattoirs there was an artists' colony known

Interior II, 1911
Oil on canvas, 100 × 180 cm
Private collection

Reclining Nude, 1911
Gouache on cardboard, 24 × 34 cm
Mr. and Mrs. Eric Estorick Collection

as 'La Ruche' (the beehive) from the shape of its central building, a dodecagonal wooden pavilion. This was one of the places that gave Paris its reputation as an art metropolis; painters and sculptors from all over the world gathered there in quest of international careers. There were nearly 140 studios there, rudimentary and dirty, but cheap; and in the winter of 1911/1912 Chagall moved into one of them. His neighbours included a number of Russians, among them Chaim Soutine, a wilful and grouchy eccentric, an Eastern Jew like Chagall. With the move, a change occurred in the format of Chagall's works; he now had more space than in his little quarters in Montmartre and was able to paint on bigger canvases. Many of the pictures he did at 'La Ruche' bear the date 1911, but in fact the artist did not date them immediately on completion, and when he did so later, looking back, he rather mixed up the chronological order of his works. For his own purposes, he grouped his œuvre into cycles which he then dated according to the promptings of some inner time-schedule which had little to do with the realities of the calendar. This may seem a trivial point, but here, too, Chagall proves a

"There in the Louvre, looking at paintings by Manet, Millet and others, I realised why my links to Russia and Russian art were so slack, why I did not even speak their language."

MARC CHAGALL in *My Life*

The Man with the Pig, 1922/23
Lithograph, 46.5 × 32.5 cm

"But perhaps my art is the art of a luna-
tic, I thought, mere glittering quicksilver,
a blue soul breaking in upon my pictures."
                    MARC CHAGALL in *My Life*

I and the Village, 1911
Oil on canvas, 191 × 150.5 cm
Museum of Modern Art, New York

master of ironic deception, affecting to despise conventions of
orderliness and only conceding allegiance to a clownish inner
world of his own.

'I and the Village' (right) is dated 1911 but was painted at 'La
Ruche'; it is Chagall's definitive programmatic painting of the
Paris years. The radial, centrifugal structure of the picture has
here become the major compositional principle. Chagall starts
out from Delaunay's use of sectional, sliced images – with the
analogy of circle and sun as a figurative element in what is an
otherwise abstract configuration of colour – and goes on to
achieve a pictorial unity through the yoking of motifs taken from
different realms of given reality. The four sections of the work are
dominated by archetypal human and animal figures as well as
Nature (in the form of a twig) and Civilisation (the village). Narra-
tion and plot are no longer needed; the geometrical arrangement,
criss-crossing the picture with diagonals and arcs, suffices to
give order to the subject. Two of Cubism's most electrifying
devices, the juxtaposition of motifs and a certain transparency in
the forms, are tested here for their ability to realise images from
memory as well as visions and fragments of the most diverse
kinds of reality in a painting. The head of the lamb, its contours
creating the space for the milking scene, houses and people
standing on their heads, and proportions contrary to all experience are arranged on associative lines and stand for a reality
beyond the visible world, for an imaginative realm in which
memories become symbols. For, indeed, all of the details in
'I and the Village' are taken from memory. The artist has availed
himself of Cubism, which places so strong an emphasis on
concrete appearance, in order to create an autonomous world
dependent on nothing but his own psychology. "Once in Paris I
was finally able to express the (somehow) culinary joy I had
sometimes felt in Russia – the joy of my childhood memories of
Vitebsk," writes Chagall. Not until he was in Paris did he find the
means to open up his own inner world, his feelings of happiness,
his longing for the little realm of his childhood.

The title 'I and the Village' is notable for its imaginative
succinctness, at odds (as it were) with the interplay of ambi-
guities in the painted scene. Like 'To my Betrothed' (p. 17) or 'To
Russia, with Asses and Others' (p. 25) the title was thought out
by Blaise Cendrars, Chagall's most important companion during
the Paris years. Compared to the distinctly rigorous intellectuality
of his fellow painters, the evocative staccato of images and the
anarchic merriness of the linguistic coinages in Cendrars's
poems and novels represented a counterpart to Chagall's
associative world of wonders. The people who supported
Chagall in his chosen approach, sharing his taste for poetry and
likewise questing for the hidden significance of things, were
literary people. "A genius, as split as a peach," Cendrars said of

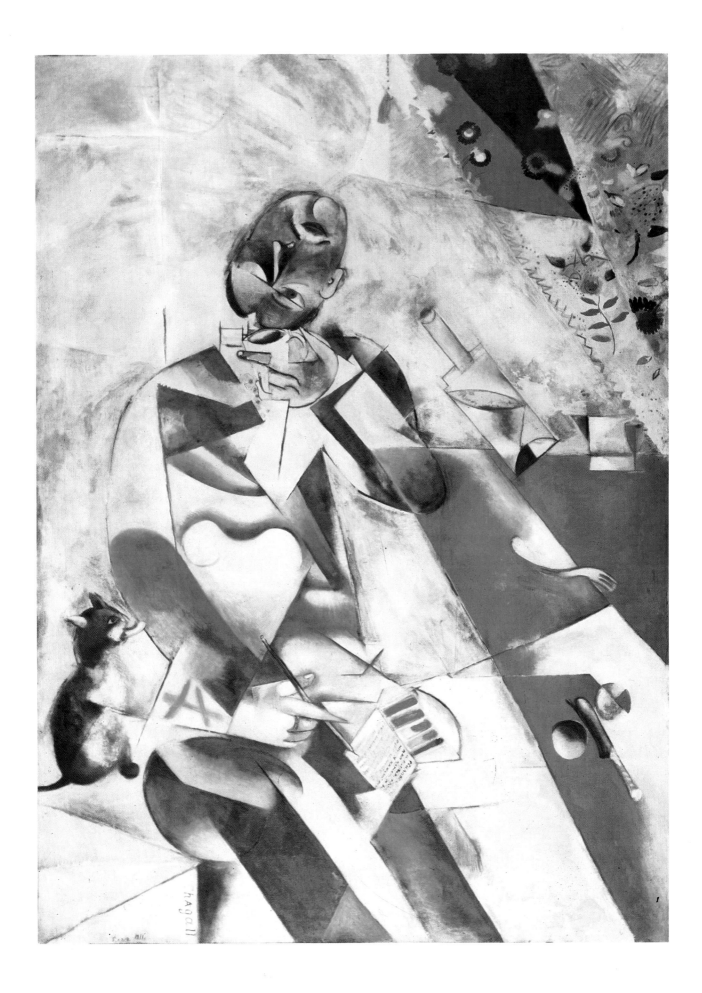

To Russia, with Asses and Others, ca. 1911/12
Oil on canvas, 156 × 122 cm
Musée National d'Art Moderne,
Centre Georges Pompidou, Paris

quest for the secrets told by things. The childhood experiences Chagall retells in his visual world are presented within the traditions of his origins as well as the anti-rational patterns of Russian thought and the strict veto on images that marked Jewish life. To this extent, Chagall's settings are never separable from a mystical, conceptual world where his motifs are transmuted into symbols that stand for some invisible reality.

The second version of 'Birth', dated 1912, indeed reveals a far freer sense of access to the mysteries of Nature (p. 28). The stiff pathos of the earlier version, where Chagall's desire for an artistic image impaired the expressive potential of the work, has gone, to be replaced by a cheerful acceptance of the story-telling urge. The young mother is still lying on her bloodstained sheets, but now she is surrounded by busy and colourful vitality: two women are conducting an excited conversation, others have nodded off at the stove, and to the right of the picture people are waiting to begin celebrating the happy event in a fit manner. The dynamics of visual shapes, introduced into Chagall's work by his borrowings from Cubism, adds a certain liveliness to the pictorial narrative. At last the childhood experiences which Chagall always made use of in his work have that vibrancy and charming vitality which, quite apart from any symbolic values, renders them accessible in the simplest of ways as an account of life. The poet's head askew on his shoulders and the soldier, holding his finger under the samovar tap and saluting, while his cap raises itself (as in 'The Soldier drinks', p. 27), are often to be seen in this period of his œuvre. The chatty tone is typical of Chagall.

As in the work of his great contemporary, Picasso, there are analytic and synthetic phases in alternation in Chagall's art. In the early Paris period, influenced by the analogous methods being applied by Cubism, Chagall explored his experiences through the interaction of motifs; he juxtaposed impressions and memories, linking them only by means of an abstract structure unifying the whole canvas space. Later in Paris he increasingly paid attention to the scene that dominated an entire picture, intensifying thought into one single moment where time appears to stand still. "Even as I was taking part in that unique upheaval in artistic techniques in France, in my own thoughts, in my soul as it were, I returned to my own country. I lived with my back turned to what was in front of me." Thus the artist described his focus on the past, writing in 1960; that return to the past was also a withdrawal from the art scene of the avant-garde, which equated artistic progress with novelty and with originality of language, both spoken or written.

'The Cattle Dealer' (p. 31), dated 1912 but (like so many of Chagall's paintings) probably done later, reproduces instead the harmonious simplicity of peasant life. Metaphors of security and well-being dominate this rural scene: the unborn foal in the

Homage to Apollinaire, 1911/12
Oil and powdered gold and silver
on canvas, 200 × 189.5 cm
Stedelijk van Abbe Museum, Eindhoven

mare's belly, the lamb on the woman's shoulders (alluding to the Christian image of the Good Shepherd), the bridge across which the cart is quietly rolling. The relaxed overall impression, created by the compositional sequence of horizontals and verticals, might lead us to forget that these animals also mean the money deals of the market place; perhaps they are on their way to be slaughtered. Recollections of his homeland gave Chagall's por-

26

trayal something of the harmless prettiness of genre painting.
'The Pinch of Snuff' (p. 30) pays still more striking homage to
the homeland. The imperious figure of the bearded, sidelocked
Jew, with phylactery and Star of David in the background and the
book with Hebrew characters, call up a familiar image, while the
colours give it the defamiliarized appearance of a vision. It is
caught between near and far, everyday and exotic, and testifies

The Soldier drinks, 1911/12
Oil on canvas, 109 × 94.5 cm
Solomon R. Guggenheim Museum,
New York

Birth, 1912
Oil on canvas, 112.5 × 193.5 cm
Art Institute of Chicago, Chicago

Right:
Adam and Eve, 1912
Oil on canvas, 160.5 × 109 cm
St. Louis Art Museum, St. Louis (Mo.)

eloquently to the artist's homesickness. The book's Hebrew lettering includes the name "Segal Mosche", the artist's own name in his home country, a name which he had internationalized, for the sake of convenience, into "Marc Chagall" when still in Russia. His wish to see the homeland once more was growing ever stronger.

In spring 1914 he got his chance. At Apollinaire's suggestion, Herwarth Walden, mentor of the Expressionists and editor of *Der Sturm,* Germany's most significant avant-garde art periodical, arranged Chagall's first major solo exhibition at his Berlin gallery. Though he had sold a few graphic works, Chagall had been doing bad business in Paris; the famous dealer's offer seemed tantamount to an international breakthrough. The irony of fate and politics decreed, however, that Chagall was to see none of the proceeds from these pictures. The outbreak of the First World War put his career back by years. "My paintings were showing off in the Potsdamer Strasse," Chagall recalled, "while nearby the cannons were being loaded." Nonetheless, on 13th June, 1914, he travelled to Russia on a visitor's visa, which was valid for three months, to attend his sister's wedding, revive memories and see Bella again. Soon frontiers were closed, and a stay he had meant to last weeks became one of eight years. Chagall had returned to the scene of almost all his paintings. 'The Fiddler' (p. 33) is one of his last Paris works. The earlier

version (p. 32), dated 1912/1913, allows the tablecloth it is painted on to show through, and in this, and in the use of mutually contradictory proportions, is squarely within the Cubist ambit; in the later version, by contrast, a twisty track curves through the canvas, lending the scene spatial and dramtic unity. The red-clad fiddler, with the beggar lad behind him, waiting for a contribution, is the dominant figure. Traditionally he leads Jewish wedding processions (compare the illustration on p. 10); we can therefore see the two people in the background as a newly-wed couple. The weighty equilibrium is scarcely disturbed any more by grotesqueness, and only the use of colour preserves those elements of the imagination which (of course) these pictures, painted in the great Western metropolis, in fact represent. 'The Fiddler' tends to obscure its own artifice and affects a veri-similitude of the portrayed elements, despite the fact that they were not painted from life. Whatever the case, the painting includes expressive approaches which Chagall, the motifs now immediately before him in Russia, would be able to re-use unchanged.

The Cattle Dealer, 1912
Oil on canvas, 97 × 200.5 cm
Kunstmuseum, Basle

LEFT:
The Pinch of Snuff, 1912
Oil on canvas, 128 × 90 cm
Private collection

PAGE 32:
The Fiddler, 1912/13
Oil on canvas, 188 × 158 cm
Stedelijk Museum, Amsterdam

PAGE 33:
The Fiddler, 1911–14
Oil on canvas, 94.5 × 69.5 cm
Kunstsammlung Nordrhein-Westfalen, Düsseldorf

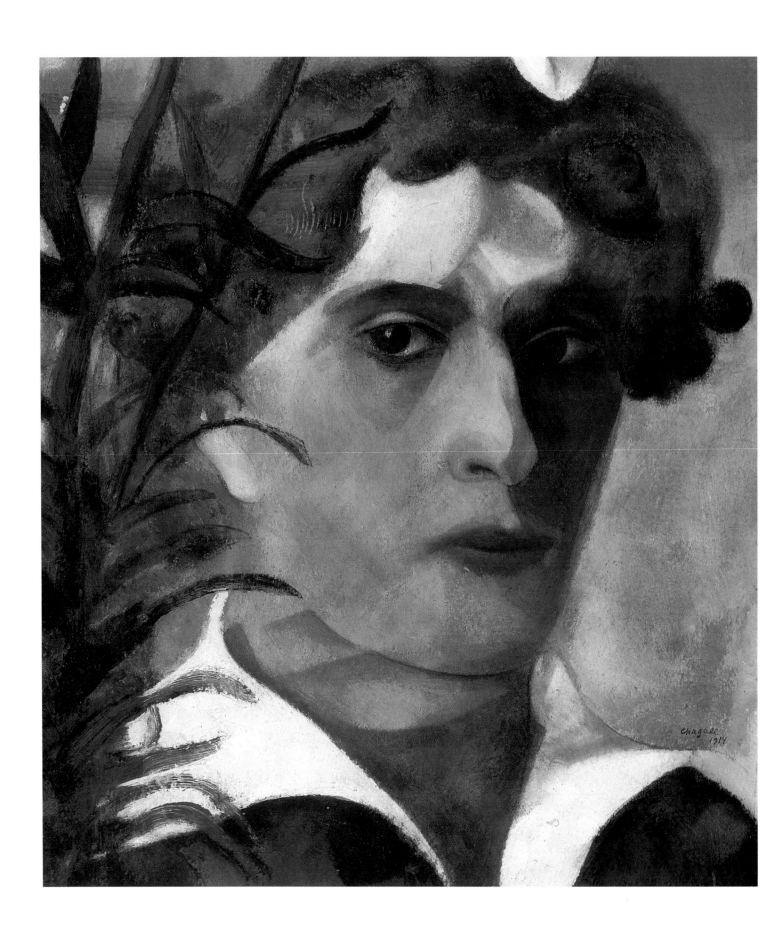

War and Revolution in Russia 1914–1923

"Vitebsk is a world all of its own, a unique town, an unhappy town, a boring town." Still, compared with what Chagall was to experience in the years ahead, his adjective "boring" might be better applied to Paris than to his home town. His stay in France was marked by constant work and the uneventful social life of elite Bohemian circles. His Paris work was inspired less by an attempt to grasp the reality of the big city than by reflection on himself, a quest for the sources of his own vitality. Now, war and revolution were to determine Chagall's life – and his art, too – and were to place him in situations of considerable existential trouble.

All pretentiousness has disappeared from the self-portrait he painted shortly after his return (left). It is a changed man the artist now shows us, compared to the similar version done in 1909 (p. 2); sceptically, almost with a touch of mystery, he peers out from the leaves of the plant, ready to hide behind them at any moment. Here Chagall emphasizes the soft, feminine features of his face. He has something of the little boy smearing rouge on his face (as he used to like doing). No doubt this painting may have corresponded to what his family expected to see, may have confirmed the image of him that had remained with them. More than that, however, the portrait documents Chagall's fear of conscription into the Czar's army. Chagall vehemently avoids even the remotest suggestion of manly strength, which might have made him the kind of wartime cannon fodder that Jews had often been felt to be good enough for.

And "woina" (war) is the sole word we can make out on the front page of 'The Smolensk Newspaper' (p. 37). The paper is on the table between two men, whose conversation appears to deal exclusively with the carnage ahead of Europe. The old Jew, resting his chin thoughtfully in his cupped hands, is thinking of the compulsory conscription Czarist regimes have been imposing on his people from time immemorial. Nor is his vis-à-vis, whose suit and hat pronounce him to be a bourgeois, at all enthusiastic either; he is seen mopping his brow in distraction. Paul Cézanne's 'Card Players' influenced this painting, but

Self-portrait, 1922/23
Lithograph, 24.5 × 18.2 cm

Self-portrait, 1914
Oil on cardboard, 30 × 26.5 cm
Philadelphia Museum of Art,
Philadelphia

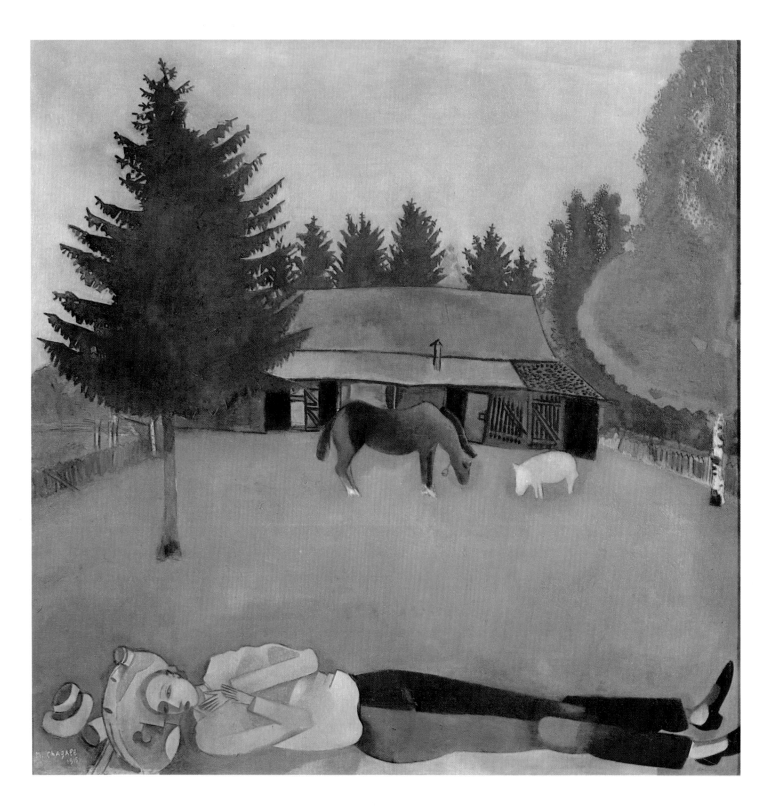

The Poet Reclining, 1915
Oil on cardboard, 77 × 77.5 cm
Tate Gallery, London

paintings, the great central image of my art." With the energies of a poet, Chagall uses words such as "flow", "haunt" or "hover" to give linguistic expression to the exhilaration and happiness he felt with Bella. The dizzy freedom from gravity we observe in the couple in the painting is, strictly speaking, simply the visual transcript twin of metaphoric language, a faithful reformulation of linguistic ideas into images in paint. The label "poetry" has time and time again been attached to Marc Chagall's art, and in this identification of written and visual language it proves apt.

The painter and his bride dreamt of carefree serenity in the country, and the picturesque idyll – lying back in the grass – became real in a painting: 'The Poet Reclining' (left) shows the poet stretched full length, matching the lower edge of the picture. Overhead, with nothing to decide whether we are seeing the poet's vision or a real scene, we see an idyll of Nature: "Alone at last in the country. Woods, pine trees, solitude. The moon behind the wood. The pig in the sty, and through the window the horse in the fields. The sky a lilac colour," Chagall recalls in *My Life*. As in the case of the poet in the painting, the autobiography gives no definite indication whether an actual experience is being described or merely the picture. What gives enduring life to poetry, that highly deliberate game played with unclarity and ambiguity, is precisely the blurring of the fictive and the real such as Chagall offers us here; and yet, however much they may toy with poeticism, these paintings are nevertheless conjurations of

The Feast of the Tabernacles, 1916
Gouache, 33 × 41 cm
Galerie Rosengart, Lucerne

"Down with Naturalism, Impressionism, and realistic Cubism . . . Let us indulge our own lunacy! What is needed is a purifying bloodbath, a revolution in the depths and not on the surface."

MARC CHAGALL

41

Bella, 1925
Etching and cold needle,
22.5 × 11.6 cm

"In the mornings and evenings she
would bring to my studio cakes she had
baked with loving care, fried fish, boiled
milk, colourful fabrics, and even boards
of wood to use as an easel. All I had to do
was open my window and in streamed
the blueness of the sky, love and flowers with her. Dressed all in white or all in
black, she has long been haunting my
paintings, the great central image of my
art."   MARC CHAGALL in *My Life*

Bella with White Collar, 1917
Oil on canvas, 149 × 72 cm
Courtesy of the artist's family

a world where all is well. They afford ways of escaping the tough
reality of the war years.

Soon, though, that reality overtook Chagall. Military service
proved unavoidable. To get out of being sent to the front, and
thus to certain injury of body and soul, Chagall took work in his
brother-in-law Jakov Rosenfeld's office in the capital, where
essential war work was being done, which rated as equivalent to
serving at the front. And so Chagall spent his days in St. Petersburg, monotonously stamping papers, disinclined to paint.

In Paris, with its own tremendously active art scene, Chagall
had learnt little of Russia's remarkable artistic evolution, of the
avant-garde's progress from regional smallness to larger international importance. In St. Petersburg he was now able to
engage in new developments. In 1912 he had participated in the
group show entitled *Donkey's Tail,* sending his painting 'The
Dead Man' from Paris; the aesthetics of that exhibition were not
unlike his own. In 1916 Chagall somewhat belatedly turned to the
Primitivism then being practised by Nathalie Gontcharova and
Michael Larionov, and the effect can be seen particularly clearly
in 'The Feast of the Tabernacles' (p. 41). Figures of a deliberate
awkwardness move across a space, angular and as if they had
been placed on a background they had not the slightest connec-
tion with. As if seen with a child's perspective, they are reduced
to complete profiles or completely frontal images; there are no
intermediate shades or nuances, since this would not fit the
robust simplicity of the scene. It is only in his rendering of the
summer house roof, with its vague gestures towards Cubism,
that Chagall demonstrates that the crude fashioning of the picture
is deliberate and not due to any lack of skill. Locked away in the
cramped and spartan confines of a war economy office, the artist
could not rise to that fleet-footed choreographic brush work that
distinguishes the paintings inspired by Bella (see right). The plain
and pithy working of 'The Feast of the Tabernacles' reflects
Chagall's emotional condition.

An event was to follow which, according to Chagall, was the
most important in his life, and which was to keep the artist, and
many more besides, in suspense for years to come. At the heart
of the nation, in the capital, he watched the signals for struggle
against the hopelessly outdated Czarist regime grow into a
revolution. During the ten days that shook the world, St. Petersburg was in the hands of the Reds. "Thus saith the Lord God:
Behold, O my people, I will open your graves, and cause you to
come up out of your graves, and bring you into the land of Israel."
These words of the vision of Ezekiel are inscribed in Hebrew
lettering above the 'Cemetery Gates' (p. 45) which Chagall
painted at that very time. A mood of turbulent change prevailed
throughout the nation, and thus Chagall's use of the Old Testament prophecy for a present rejoicing in its future by no means

The Artist's Father's Grave, 1922
Leaf 19 in the series 'My Life',
cold needle etching, 10.8 × 14.9 cm

"Clad in a Russian smock, a leather
briefcase under my arm, I gave the perfect impression of a Soviet functionary."

MARC CHAGALL in *My Life*

Cemetery Gates, 1917
Oil on canvas, 87 × 68.6 cm
Private collection

seems blasphemous. The Bolsheviks had taken Russia out of the war, and the Jews at long last had equal citizens' rights with other Russians. The early days of the Revolution were marked by untroubled optimism.

Lenin appointed Anatoli Lunacharski head of his Ministry of Culture. Chagall had known Lunacharski in Paris, where the émigré was making his living as a journalist, writing for Russian-language publications. In September 1918, this acquaintance-ship resulted in an official position for Chagall: he was made Fine Arts Commissar in Vitebsk. Art was highly valued in the opening phase of the Revolution, and it was hoped that aesthetics and politics would inspire each other in their strivings for a more human future. Communists saw both art and their conception of the state as being opposed to bourgeois attitudes, as being interdependent, and (by virtue of being progressive and avant-garde) as offering them the chance of a better world. The old dream of art autonomously practised for its own sake was to be replaced by an art engaged with reality.

Chagall, full of enthusiasm, plunged headlong into his new position as a professional aesthetician; he organized exhibitions, opened museums, and restarted classes at the Vitebsk Academy of Art. And presently this confirmed individualist and resolute advocate of the strange and unusual was to be found putting the case for the power of anonymity and equality: "Believe me, the working people, once they have been transformed, will be ready to storm the heights of art and culture." Chagall was quite the Communist, without reservation.

Chagall planned to mark the first anniversary of the Revolu-tion with colourful celebratory decorations all over Vitebsk. Although he largely kept to the decreed ideology in such works as 'War on the Palaces', the reaction of orthodox comrades was unanimous: "Why is the cow green and why is the horse flying in the sky?" they asked, puzzled, according to Chagall. "What has it got to do with Marx and Lenin?" The painter had scarcely begun to identify with his new cause when he was confronted with bull-headed demands for the political applicability of his art. 'The Painter: To the Moon' (p. 47), dated 1917 by Chagall but very likely done no earlier than 1919, is Chagall's response, and stubbornly insists on artistic inspiration. The familiar figure of the painter reflectively lost in his dreams hovers through the picture, removed from this world into a sphere of imaginary and (as it were) heavenly rapture. His head is crowned with laurels; this ages-old symbol of the poet's fame is meant as an eloquent testimony to the painter's intention to create realities of his own.

Not least because Vitebsk was largely spared the terrible food shortages that soon ravaged the land, the Academy of Art, under its director Chagall, soon had an impressive list of famous teachers on its staff. One by one, the crème of the Russian avant-

Peasant Life (The Stable; Night; Man with Whip), 1917
Oil on cardboard, 21 × 21.5 cm
Solomon R. Guggenheim Museum,
New York

garde moved to the provinces, and illustrious names such as El Lissitzky and Kasimir Malevich brought an air of Bohemianism to Vitebsk. Soon, conflicts over the direction true art had to take began to jeopardize Chagall's future. In 1915 Malevich had caused a sensation with his 'Black Square on a White Ground', and had become established internationally as one of the leaders of the new art. The cerebral equilibrium of abstract zones of colour which Malevich advocated in the name of "pure painting", and his thesis that art should abandon all links with given reality, were thorns in Chagall's flesh. While Chagall was away on a trip to Moscow he was deposed by a palace revolution, and the free academy was declared a Suprematist institute. True, Chagall was restored to both his office and his esteem on his return; but he had conceived a deep distrust of the Revolution and its notion of art. In May 1920 Chagall quit Vitebsk, and moved with his family to Moscow.

Still, even he had not kept totally free of Malevich's influence. 'Peasant Life' (left), dated 1917 and in fact done in 1919 in Vitebsk, clearly evidences a link with Malevich's programme with its meditative balance of monochrome geometrical shapes. But

The Painter: To the Moon, 1917
Gouache and water-colour on paper,
32 × 30 cm
Marcus Diener Collection, Basle

The Musician, 1922
Additional leaf in the series 'My Life',
cold needle etching, 27.5 × 21.6 cm

Chagall has peopled this abstract grid with his usual personnel and re-interpreted the colour fields in terms of areas of real life; the man with the whip and the woman with the animal occupy these zones in archetypal confrontation. This peaceful geometrical order, which served Malevich as a metaphor for the inner world of thought and feeling, is transformed under Chagall's brush into a concrete basic idea, a core repertoire of motifs for the execution of genre scenes.

The family led their life in the new capital in considerable poverty. Chagall was fond of the stage, and created designs for Moscow's Jewish Theatre, but he earned only enough for the bare essentials. He made monumental murals for the foyer and auditorium, with allegorical images of aspects of theatre; 'Green Violinist' (right), painted in 1923/24, is a replica of the mural depicting Music, and a faithful reduced-size version of an original in the Moscow theatre.

The familiar figure of the fiddler has lost none of its suggestive power for Chagall, and the image conjures forth another realm at a time of deep depression.

The support the state gave artists was scaled according to the political usefulness of their works. Chagall was placed very far down in the grant hierarchy, since none other than Malevich was responsible for classifying artists, and Malevich had a low opinion of his fellow artist. "I think the Revolution could be a great thing if it retained its respect for what is other and different," wrote Chagall in *My Life,* which he was completing at the time. It was this respect, a respect for his own affection for the unusual, that he felt a lack of in the new order; the totalitarian tendency to steamroll everything level had left his appeals to the power of fantasy unheeded. With neither money, success or prospects, Chagall no longer had any reason to stay in the nation which was now known as the Soviet Union. Lunacharski got the family a passport so that they could leave.

Chagall now recollected Walden, the Berlin gallery owner, and the success he had been denied for so many years. He planned to pick up threads in Berlin and re-establish a secure finanical footing for his career by selling paintings there; when he arrived in the city in summer 1922, it turned out that his name did indeed have some currency. Walden had sold the pictures Chagall had left in Berlin and had paid the money into an account for the artist. However, high inflation had now hit Germany and the money had become valueless, so that Chagall found himself with neither pictures nor funds. He went to court over the matter, and a few of the paintings, hastily bought back, were restored to him by way of compensation. But he literally had to start all over again.

The Green Violinist, 1923/24
Oil on canvas, 198 × 108.6 cm
Solomon R. Guggenheim Museum,
New York

France and America
1923–1948

Chagall's memoirs in *My Life,* finished in 1922, make best sense read with the upheaval and removal from Moscow to Paris in mind. Not yet forty, the artist took an autobiographical retrospective look at a past which had been far from uneventful and tried to draw up a balance sheet on his own life. The gentle irony which turns the autonomous world of his paintings into the diary-like impressions of childhood is also to be found in these recollections. His art was lost in the gutters of the market, but his recollections were still all there.

The book was meant to be published by Paul Cassirer in Berlin and was also intended to serve as a sign of life for his old friends in France. But for the time being only a portfolio of twenty etchings (Chagall's illustrations to the text) was produced; the book edition was not published until 1931 in Paris, Bella having translated it from Russian into French. Still, the great Parisian dealer Ambroise Vollard, mentor of the Cubists and a friendly father-figure to Picasso in particular, commissioned Chagall to illustrate Nikolai Gogol's *Dead Souls,* and on 1st September, 1923, Chagall left for Paris and a new artistic career.

"What I first set eyes on was a trough. Simple, massive, semi-hollow, semi-oval. A junkshop trough. Once I got in, I filled it completely." These are the opening words of *My Life.* 'The Watering Trough' (p. 52) recalls the memoirs' opening and emblematically emphasizes Chagall's continuing ties to past times he could not break loose from. Perhaps working on the book by his fellow countryman, Gogol revived his recollections of Russia; at any rate, as his fame increased, this kind of subject matter came to be his trademark, with Chagall was not so much focussing attention on the world of the *shtetl* as quoting himself. The woman and the pig are both bending over the trough in unison. They have the same long backs, their heads are in the same profile position, they both need water: tongue-in-cheek, the artist is pointing out the affinity of human and animal. The scene has its own unity, and in its absurdity has the flavour of the earlier genre scenes observed from further away; the fine, subtle colouring,

The Walk, 1922
Additional leaf in the series 'My Life',
cold needle etching, 25 × 19 cm

The Three Acrobats, 1926
Oil on canvas, 117 × 89 cm
Private collection

51

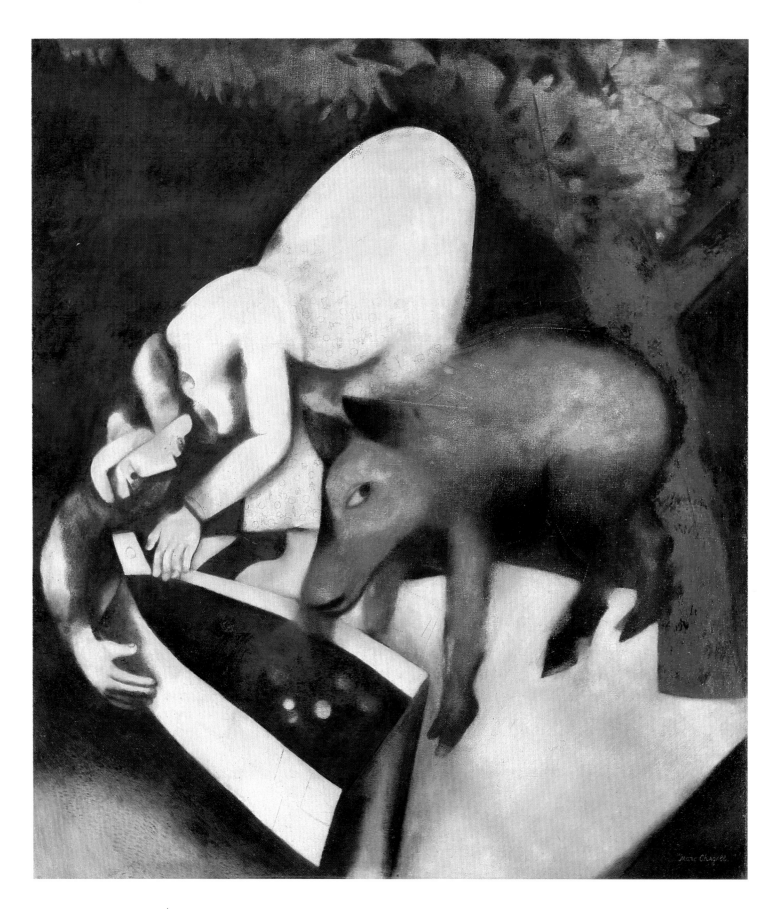

The Watering Trough, 1925
Oil on canvas, 99.5 × 88.5 cm
Philadelphia Museum of Art,
Philadelphia

with its unmistakably French character, contributes to this unity.
There are two versions of this painting, their colour schemes
quite distinct. A typically Western feeling for the emotive qualities
of colouring is superimposed atmospherically onto the earthy

subject matter drawn from Chagall's homeland. It was a strategy Chagall was to perfect in the years ahead.

In the early phase of this new Paris period, Chagall was especially fond of making two versions of a painting, as if by

Peasant Life, 1925
Oil on canvas, 101 × 80 cm
Albright-Knox Art Gallery, Buffalo (N.Y.)

The Cock and the Pearl, ca. 1927–30
Table 11 in the illustrations
for the *Fables* of La Fontaine
(published 1952)
Etching, 30.2 × 22.8 cm

creating it in duplicate he could guarantee his own existence against the predatory machinations of the market. He also set about re-doing some of the paintings that had gone missing, using reproductions or working from memory. What prompted him to these repetitive labours may have been not only the wish to repair the ravages of war and make good the loss to his art, but also a sense that, with the paintings, a part of himself had been lost.

This is by no means an inflated stylization of himself. Rather, it reflects a profound faith in the power of images, a faith that had led the Jews to veto image-making, particularly religious ones. A veto and a cult are two sides of the same coin: Chagall the Jew proves in this to be deeply rooted in his people's traditions. The ancient magic power of pictures, which Chagall liked to describe with the untranslatable word "chimie", lives on in the artist's refusal to make saleable objects of his works. He could adapt to his audience's wishes and needs in a way most of his fellow artists were unable to do, but it was an adaptability that respected the autonomous authority of the finished painting.

The subject matter of 'I and the Village' (p. 21), one of the paintings Chagall made a second copy of, re-appears in the 1925 work 'Peasant Life' (p. 53). Once again we see archetypal figures which personify a quality of simplicity in a visionary setting: human and animal figures, and a sense of idyllic security, constitute the genre's *sine qua non.* However, the geometrical grid that made the juxtapositions in the earlier painting possible has now been replaced, in compositional terms, by a principle of free association. The man feeding the horse, whose profile is the base of the house, now have a complementary rather than contrastive effect.

What inspired this painting was not so much rustic life in Russia (which Chagall, after the things he had experienced during the Revolution, was less prepared to glamourize than he had been previously) as an image Chagall had of himself. The atmospheric content of the colour scheme, and the relaxation of the strict grid, are a commentary on his own early period, viewed from the vantage point of the latest aesthetic trends. Surrealism had replaced Cubism, and Chagall felt an affinity through the liberation from self-imposed patterns of order and the reckless espousal of the kind of disorder that is typical of dreams.

"Chagall, and only Chagall, provided painting with the triumphant advent of metaphor." Thus André Breton, singing Chagall's praises, and eulogizing his poetic qualities, as late as 1945. Nevertheless, Chagall's relationship to the Surrealists was torn, whatever their theoretician-in-chief might say. Long before them, impelled by the elemental power of his homeland's folk art, he had discovered the significance of dreams, visions and the non-rational for his own work. The Surrealists, whose anti-

The Rooster, 1929
Oil on canvas, 81 × 65 cm
Thyssen-Bornemisza Collection,
Lugano-Castagnola

rational approach to art drew upon similar sources, repeatedly tried to win Chagall over, but Chagall saw their homage to the power of the unconscious as a way of pandering to the currents of taste and a wilful parade of illogicality, and was unable to identify with them. His artistic credo came straight from the heart: "The entire world within us is reality, perhaps more real than the visible world. If one calls everything that seems illogical fantasy or a fairy tale, all one proves is that one has not understood Nature." To be attached to one's dreams and yet to advocate reality constituted no contradiction in Chagall's eyes.

The family lived in the Avenue d'Orléans, in the apartment where Lenin had stayed before them. The rooms, crammed with the magic of oriental décor, were an oasis of the exotic in the cool atmosphere of the big city. They were dominated by carpets and cushions, and the ambience matched Chagall's public image; the aura of the unfamiliar and mysterious which his pictorial images evoked increasingly extended to the artist himself, and became a means of publicizing himself which came to accompany every step in his career.

In 1924 the first Chagall retrospective was seen in Paris, and in 1926 he had his first New York exhibition. From the mid-1920s, at the latest, the provincial Russian's visions had become public property; and both in his life-style and in his work, subtle changes in the direction of his wider audience's taste began to become apparent.

In 'The Three Acrobats' (p. 50) the central figure leaps forward, with a final athletic motion, to receive applause and bouquets at the edge of the stage. Chagall had always loved the dreamy world of the circus and had been enthralled by the blend of dance, theatre, music and language. This painting (done in 1926) is the earliest of Chagall's works with the circus as subject. It took him a relatively long time to express in paint a subject he had long been inclined towards and the explanation may lie in the pressure he was now under to adapt. For the first time he now seemed willing to apply his visionary visual terms to a realm of experience where a visionary quality was natural and, in any case, characteristic. The magic of the motif and that of the artistic strategy now met, and threatened to cancel each other out. Where Picasso had mercilessly confronted his tumblers and harlequins with reality, Chagall's pictures of acrobats have problems with tautology.

Not only the subject but also the clarity and near-classical coolness of the presentation remind of us of the great Spanish painter. The framing of the central figure by the smaller flanking ones, the echoing of this triangular composition by the canopy-like curtain, the robust physicality of the figures (with an effect like statues), create an almost academic repose which reflects a centuries-old code of beauty. The figurative emphasis is now on

TO MARC CHAGALL

"Ass or cow rooster or horse
Through to the body of a fiddle
Singing man a single bird
Nimbly dancing with his wife

A couple immersed in spring

Gold of the grass lead of the sky
Marked off by blue flames
By the freshness of the dew
The blood shimmers the heart beats

A couple the first reflection

And in a vaulted dome of snow
The full vine sketches in
A face with lips of moonlight
That never sleeps at night."

PAUL ELUARD

Lovers in the Lilacs, 1930
Oil on canvas, 128 × 87 cm
Richard S. Zeisler Collection, New York

Three Acrobats, 1926
Etching and aquatint, 34.2 × 37.3 cm

artistic virtuosity as assessed by the touchstone of pictorial tradition; the chaos of visions clamouring for expression has been ousted in favour of the timeless norm of classic simplicity. The painting has all the atmosphere characteristic of Chagall's work, but also a highly elaborate, even overdone touch of the Old Masters.

In his biography of Chagall, Franz Meyer quotes an aphorism that sums up the two artists: "Picasso stood for the triumph of the intellect, Chagall for the glory of the heart." The two now established a relaxed friendship.

The dreamy elegance of the loving couple in 'The Rooster' (p. 55), where the monumental bird has replaced the lover, belongs in that twilit world that can be grasped only in terms of mood and emotion. The bliss these two are enjoying is shared by two other couples, who are secluded in the background of the painting and in the security of their affections.

The love poetry written by Chagall in such works, and the tender elation (which matched his own emotional situation), peaks in 'Lovers in the Lilacs' (p. 56), painted in 1930. The couple, idyllically bedded down in a giant bouquet, are wholly immersed in the timelessness of love. Following an ages-old pictorial code, Chagall has here incorporated two of his central motifs: an icon showing the *Madonna Platytera* was his inspiration, a representation of the pregnant Virgin Mary with the child painted on her belly for clarity's sake. In painting the mare with the foal in her womb (cf. 'The Cattle Dealer', p. 31) Chagall had already echoed this treatment; now he abstracted it into an explanation of the symbolic dimension that was always in his motifs. Without doubt, this approach simplified the business of decoding his pictorial messages, and helped Chagall to the popularity his work enjoyed at the time, but at the same time the wish to be comprehensible lent the paintings a touch of Romanticism that seemed somewhat out-of-date.

Yet, that first decade in Paris, as the artist tells us, was "the happiest time of my life". A contract with the art dealer Bernheim removed his financial worries, the family was able to move into a villa, and soon they were taking their summer holidays in the south of France for granted. This more lavish way of life, this private happiness, was accompanied by a compulsive turn to the opulent in Chagall's work: the carefree naivety of the pictures reflects the painter's own untroubled existence, and the magical atmosphere replaces that liveliness of subject matter which requires an eventful reality as a corrective.

His mood, however, was shortly to darken. In a 1933 painting entitled 'Solitude' (p. 60), the merry dance of loving couples is ousted by profound melancholy. Lost in contemplation, cloaked in his tallith, a full-bearded Jew of indeterminate age is sitting in the grass, the scrolls of the Torah unopened in his left

The Acrobat, 1930
Oil on canvas, 65 × 32 cm
Musée National d'Art Moderne,
Centre Georges Pompidou, Paris

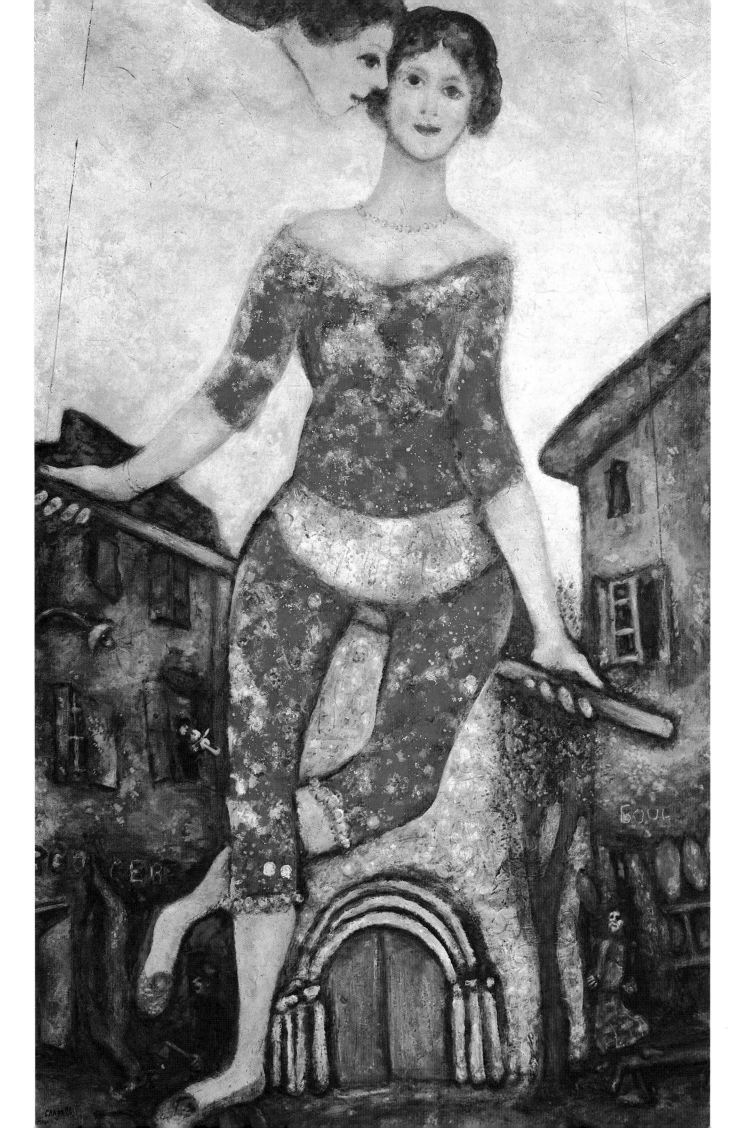

hand: the religious tradition of his forefathers affords no balm for his misery, it seems. The sad-eyed cow lying beside him recalls the words of the prophet Hosea: "For Israel slideth back as a back-sliding heifer." (Hosea 4,16.) These figures symbolize the people of the Jewish diaspora, Chagall's people (as the Russian surroundings imply). The picturesque old man can be seen as Ahasverus, the eternal Wandering Jew, roaming the world in uncertainty as to his future. On the horizon, beyond a countryside which is on the whole seen with tender affection, storm clouds are gathering, and their blackness is threatening the angel in the sky.

In 1931 Chagall had visited Palestine, the Promised Land, but in his pictures the result of his travels appears as anything but optimism. Alert to the world he lived in, Chagall recorded notes of discord and unease: the year that saw the barbaric ideology of National Socialism triumphant in Germany also saw repose driven out of Chagall's paintings by a real world of harsh power.

In 'Solitude', Chagall was still using motifs that were very much his own to indicate dangers that were menacing himself, his people, and all of Europe. It was not the narrative content of the painting, but its atmosphere that conveyed his newly gloomy

Solitude, 1933
Oil on canvas, 102 × 169 cm
Tel Aviv Museum, Tel Aviv

The Revolution, 1937
Oil on canvas, 50 × 100 cm
Courtesy of the artist's family

view of the world; in this respect, it resembled the mood paintings of the 1920s. Another journey, to Poland in spring 1935, finally convinced Chagall that a new political reality had come to the fore which his own world of images could no longer ignore: he was deeply affected by what he saw in the Warsaw ghetto, and was present when his friend Dubnow was called a "dirty Jew" in the street. The world of the Jews was no longer a dreamy, cosy sanctum of timeless contentment, but was instead being perverted into a scene of rabid pogroms and racist obsession. And the presence of this existential threat restored the authentic power to Chagall's work.

Fascist assaults on the very core of human morality had been answered by Picasso in what ranks as the finest product of committed historical art in the twentieth century. His 'Guernica' (Museo del Prado, Madrid) expressed the full depth of protest that civilization was compelled to make when confronted with political cynicism, and in 1937 the painting was (sadly enough) a major attraction at the World Exhibition in Paris. That same year, Chagall documented his own commitment in 'The Revolution' (above), an elegiac work to match the Spanish artist's direct accusation. Chagall's painting is not a response to a specific event, but an attempt to articulate political disquiet and unease in his own terms. Two ways of grasping or shaping the world are juxtaposed in antithesis. To the left, revolutionaries are seen rushing the barricades, their red flags proudly proclaiming the victory of Communism. To the right, this image of unity, standing for political demands for equality, is counterbalanced by the free play of the human imagination. We see musicians, clowns and

"I came to Palestine to examine certain ideas, and I came without a camera, without even a brush. No documentation, no tourist impressions, and nevertheless I am glad to have been there. From far and wide they pour towards the Wailing Wall, bearded Jews in yellow, blue and red robes and with fur caps. Nowhere else do you see so much despair and so much joy; nowhere else are you so shaken and yet so happy as at the sight of this thousand-year-old heap of stones and dust in Jerusalem, in Sefad, in the hills where prophets upon prophets lie buried."
MARC CHAGALL

The Crucifixion, 1951/52
Lithograph, 42.3 × 33.5 cm

"What counts is art, painting, a kind of painting that is quite different from what everyone makes it out to be. But what kind? Will God or someone else give me the strength to breathe the breath of prayer and mourning into my paintings, the breath of prayer for redemption and resurrection?" MARC CHAGALL in *My Life*

White Crucifixion, 1938
Oil on canvas, 155 × 140 cm
Art Institute of Chicago, Chicago

animals playing, the customary loving couple are lolling on the roof of a wooden hut, and in typical Chagall style, the force of gravity has been suspended so that the ubiquitous energies may develop freely. The figure of Lenin links the two zones; balanced acrobatically on one hand, he is showing the revolutionaries the true way to a world of individuality.

"I think the Revolution could be a great thing if it retained its respect for what is other and different," Chagall had written, summing up his Russian experiences in the light of his view of himself as artist. The creative power of the individual is the driving force in the struggle for political liberty. But the old Jew in 'Solitude' still sits thinking about his own future and that of his people...

The painting is vehemently programmatic, and overloaded with significance, so that its capacity for atmosphere and mood has been lost. Its ambitious attempt to find a general, supra-individual relevance and its unsatisfying treatment of the technical problems remind us of Chagall's zeal in his early works: the juxtaposition of archetypes, of symbolically laden shorthand images of the world, is not equal to the task of rendering the complexity of events. Nor was Chagall himself ever satisfied with this answer to Picasso's great masterpiece. In 1943 he was to redo the large-format version of 'The Revolution' in three panels, blending the political and religious symbolism in the form of a triptych. The smaller version reproduced here was preserved to testify to the artist's direct involvement with world events (quite distinct from the wish to create timeless works of art).

The second programmatic painting of this period, 'White Crucifixion' (right), was done in 1938 and solves the problem better. In 1933, Chagall had described his aesthetic aims in these words: "If a painter is a Jew and paints life, how is he to keep Jewish elements out of his work! But if he is a good painter, his painting will contain a great deal more. The Jewish content will be there, of course, but his art will aim at universal relevance." In the figure of Christ on the cross, symbolizing the passion of the prophet of the Jews and the death of the Christian God who took on the form of a man, Chagall located a universal emblem for the sufferings of this time. Like the *arma Christi,* or the tools and implements shown in traditional crucifixion scenes, images of confusion are grouped about the cross. Revolutionary hordes with red flags rampage through a village, looting and burning houses. Refugees in a boat shout for help and gesticulate wildly. A man in Nazi uniform is desecrating a synagogue. Distressed figures in the foreground are trying to escape. Ahasverus, the Wandering Jew, is passing by in silence, stepping over a burning Torah scroll. Old Testament figures are seen hovering, lamenting against the background of desolate darkness. Still, a bright beam of light breaks in from on high, illuminating the white and

unblemished figure on the cross. All trace of his suffering is gone, and worship of his centuries-old authority is seen as a path of hope amid the traumatic events of the present day. Belief in him, so Chagall says, can move the mountains of despair.

Even the gentlest of irony has been eliminated from this picture. Naked existential fear is seen appealing pathetically to the saving power of religion in a way that is unique in Chagall's work. In this painting, and perhaps nowhere else, Chagall's recourse to the traditional repertoire of tricks is quite free of willful cleverness, and in its very use of scenes of the times, the picture becomes an integrated whole and achieves the timeless depth of an icon. "It is not right to paint pictures with symbols. If a work of art has total authenticity, symbolic meaning will be contained in it of its own accord," Chagall once said. His counterpart to Picasso's historical painting 'Guernica', which speaks of suffering, is the devotional painting 'White Crucifixion', which feels its way into that suffering.

If Chagall had been so sensitively alert to coming horror even before the outbreak of war, once war was declared his feelings became panic-stricken. To be an inner émigré, and flee the demands of political reality by withdrawing into a confined inner realm of art (as Picasso did in Paris, for example), would have meant idly waiting for the death camps. So it was that in spring 1940 he and his family moved to Gordes in the Provence, where the sheer distance from Nazi Germany guaranteed them a certain safety.

In Gordes, Chagall completed 'The Three Candles' (left) in 1940, after having worked at it for two years. Isolated from cultural life and in constant fear of internment, he reviewed his repertoire of images in a quite manic manner: the artiste, the loving couple and the village, mutely available to the painter, consolidate his safety from danger. Melancholy colours predominate, and the fearfulness expressed in the timid gestures of the figures acquires a still-life rigidity, like an emblem of transience, and is transfigured by the death symbolism of the candles into a sombre *memento mori*.

The French government came to an agreement with the Nazis and France could no longer be considered safe for Chagall. He was even seized during a raid in Marseilles and threatened with being handed over to the Germans, but American intervention rescued him. While vast numbers of his people were setting off on the tragic journey to destruction, the famous painter was able to rely on public help. On 7th May, Chagall and his family embarked for the United States. The myth of the Wandering Jew, of Jewry restlessly on the move, so often spoken of in his paintings, was no longer merely a literary motif.

On 23rd June, 1941, the day Germany attacked the USSR, Chagall arrived in New York. After Paris and Berlin he now lived in

The Three Candles, 1938–40
Oil on canvas, 127.5 × 96.5 cm
Private collection

"If ever there was a moral crisis it was that of paint, matter, blood, and all their constituents, the words and the tones, all the things one makes a work of art out of, just as one makes a life. For even if you cover a canvas with thick masses of paint, irrespective of whether the outlines of shapes can be made out or not, and even if you enlist the help of words and tones, it does not necessarily follow that an authentic work of art will have been created." MARC CHAGALL

PAGES 66/67:
L'Obsession, 1943
Oil on canvas, 77 × 108 cm
Courtesy of the artist's family

the third great metropolitan melting-pot. True to his own experience, Chagall was always attracted to great cities, where diverse and exotic peoples and cultures met; they were the elixir of life to him. The family moved into a country house at Preston (Connecticut), some way out of the city, before moving into a small New York apartment.

Responding to the events of the war from a distance but with sympathy, Chagall modulated the deeply melancholy basic tone of his last French paintings in the years that followed. War and crucifixion dominated his subject matter, but the empathic intensity was somewhat diminished. It was as if the daily news of atrocities blunted Chagall's sentimental willingness to feel solidarity.

At all events, 'L'Obsession' (pp. 66/67), painted in 1943, testifies to the impossibility of finding new images of concern, year in, year out. The flames pouring from the hut, the Jew with the three-branched candelabrum, the motif of flight in a cart, the menacingly fiery colours have the banality of quotations from himself, and only in the toppled crucifix, speaking of shattered hopes, does Chagall find a way of indicating the tremendous horrors of recent years. Nonetheless, the device has something too anecdotally trivial about it, and the linking of the passion and war is now too familiar to add any new dimension of pictorial sympathy to the powerful 'White Crucifixion'.

This suggests one of the fundamental problems of Chagall's pictorial language: a tendency for motifs to acquire an independent existence of their own, which threatens to rob them of their expressive power. Familiar elements in his work – all the loving couples, huts, animals, and later the religious images – are deployed in new combinations to determine the character of any given painting. Like words, they are strung together into ever-new sentences, yet the many repetitions deprive them of specific meaning. Their symbolic value as representatives of another reality in a picture is levelled out; instead they become quotations from Chagall's own œuvre. Parts of a seemingly mysterious world, they soon come to suggest nothing but their own exoticism, and the reality they are supposed to stand for becomes schematized.

Thus, in the end a Chagall painting will convey only a mood, a mood which depends far more on the use of colour than on exact content. The motifs merely serve a purpose of recognition, endowing the typical Chagall hallmark; and in this way Chagall's initial aura of strangeness is dispelled. The uniquely formulated appeal for tolerance and understanding became in danger of being submerged in a welter of the merely typical, and it was only Chagall's dynamic capacity for stylistic change that enabled him to keep this danger at arm's length. In this he shows himself to have been a diligent student of abstract painting: his brush-

Listening to the Cock, 1944
Oil on canvas, 92.5 × 74.5 cm
Katherine Smith Miller and
Lance Smith Miller Collection

"If in some painting I have cut off the head of a cow and replaced it upside down or have sometimes even painted the whole picture topsy-turvy, the reason was not that I wanted to create literature. I am out to introduce a psychic shock into my painting, one that is always motivated by pictorial reasoning: that is to say, a fourth dimension. An example: a street. Matisse constructs it in the spirit of Cézanne, Picasso in that of Negroes or Egyptians. I go about it differently. I have my street. In that street I place a corpse. The corpse causes psychic confusion in the street. I put a musician on a rooftop. The presence of the musician interacts with that of the corpse. Then a man sweeping the street. The image of the street-sweeper affects that of the musician. A bouquet of flowers falling down, and so forth. In this way I admit a psychic fourth dimension into pictorial representation and the two are mingled."   MARC CHAGALL

The Wedding, 1944
Oil on canvas, 99 × 74 cm
Ida Chagall Collection

strokes and combinations of colours are the major determinations of specific content and individuality in a Chagall painting, not the thematic motifs.

'The House with the Green Eye' (p. 72) and 'Madonna with the Sleigh' (p. 75) and above all 'Listening to the Cock' (p. 69) testify to this. The figure of the cockerel, distinguished from the red background only by its outline and the colourful head, incorporates two more of Chagall's exemplary motifs: the dainty position of the legs recalls the athleticism of his acrobats, while a fiddler can be found tucked away in the cock's tail-feathers. Wittily, Chagall has his cock ready to lay an egg, this image offering the same unison of male and female seen in the cow against a black background, whose head turns out to be the faces of two lovers. The crescent moon, the tree standing on its head, and the hut round off this selection of Chagall's stock imagery. The ruddy dawn heralded by the cock's crow is gradually dispelling night, the province of the lovers, and this may suggest that the picture is to be read as a document of new hope, that gleam of hope Chagall felt as the collapse of Nazism approached.

"The darkness has gathered before my eyes," reads the despairing final sentence that Chagall added to Bella's book, *First Encounter.* When it was first published, in 1947, she had already been dead for three years. She had died in mysterious circumstances, of a viral infection, and all the signs that seemed to betoken a better world had gone. The muse Chagall had so often appealed to left her book as a testament, as a final spur for her husband's work.

'The Wedding' (right), painted shortly after her death in 1944, shows the artist retelling an episode from *First Encounter,* the marriage of Bella's brother Aaron; yet the light, exhilarated tone of Bella's account, which (like her husband's autobiography) is marked by a mood of lightheartedness and playful irony, has been displaced by sinister melancholy. Bride and groom incline towards each other almost apathetically, and the angelic musicians might well be playing a death march as a wedding dance. Private grief had been added to the fateful course of world events and Chagall's pictures at this time all centre upon the death of Bella.

After the liberation of Europe, Chagall ventured back into the Old World, where his career had begun for the first time in 1946. The tentatively cheerful note struck in paintings such as 'Cow with Parasol' (p. 73) may derive from impressions of the return visit to Paris. A hot sun is burning in the sky, but the parasol promises relief . . . relief for the cow! The artist has adopted the classic stylistic device of substitution, replacing man with an animal: it is a device that is characteristic of Chagall's art, and is used in exemplary fashion in this painting, where it contributes a great deal to the anecdotal charm that is at the core of the

The House with the Green Eye, 1944
Oil on canvas, 58 × 51 cm
Ida Chagall Collection

picture's irony. Nonetheless, sombre colours still dominate the painting, and its humoresque qualities seem to be a compulsive insistence on cheerfulness.

With 'The Falling Angel' (p. 74), Chagall painted a last farewell to twenty-five years of artistic creativity, and the work represents both the essence of his committed involvement with the outside world and also his last word on a chronicle of increasing barbarity. It had taken Chagall twenty-five tormented years to complete the painting.

When he began it in 1922, with memories of the Russian revolution still fresh, the picture was to have included only the figures of the Jew and the angel and was meant as a representation of the Old Testament vindication of the presence of Evil in the world. Yet, in the years up to the painting's completion in 1947 the artist increasingly incorporated motifs reminiscent of his little Russian world, in the end even adding the Christian images of the Madonna and of Christ on the Cross. His Jewish vision, his personal life-story, and motifs of Christian redemption are incorporated into a programmatic statement that sums up Chagall's

Cow with Parasol, 1946
Oil on canvas, 77.5 × 106 cm
Richard S. Zeisler Collection, New York

"When Chagall paints you do not know if he is asleep or awake. Somewhere or other inside his head there must be an angel." PABLO PICASSO

The Falling Angel, 1923–47
Oil on canvas, 148 × 189 cm
Kunstmuseum, Basle

RIGHT:
Madonna with the Sleigh, 1947
Oil on canvas, 97 × 80 cm
Stedelijk Museum, Amsterdam

entire œuvre. The images have been added one to another; in their totality, and in the diversity of their associations, they represent Chagall's unceasing endeavour to locate one single, truthful, universally valid visual formula. Its very history, its long journey halfway round the world, the whole generation required for its completion make this picture typical of twentieth century art, of the displacement and jeopardy that beset a work in its newly autonomous condition.

Its very history gave this picture that authority which Chagall had always aimed at and which was commensurate with the Jewish awe of images. His own odyssey, which ended happily with his final return to France in summer 1948, had from a very early stage, ever since Walden's Berlin exhibition, also been the odyssey of his work.

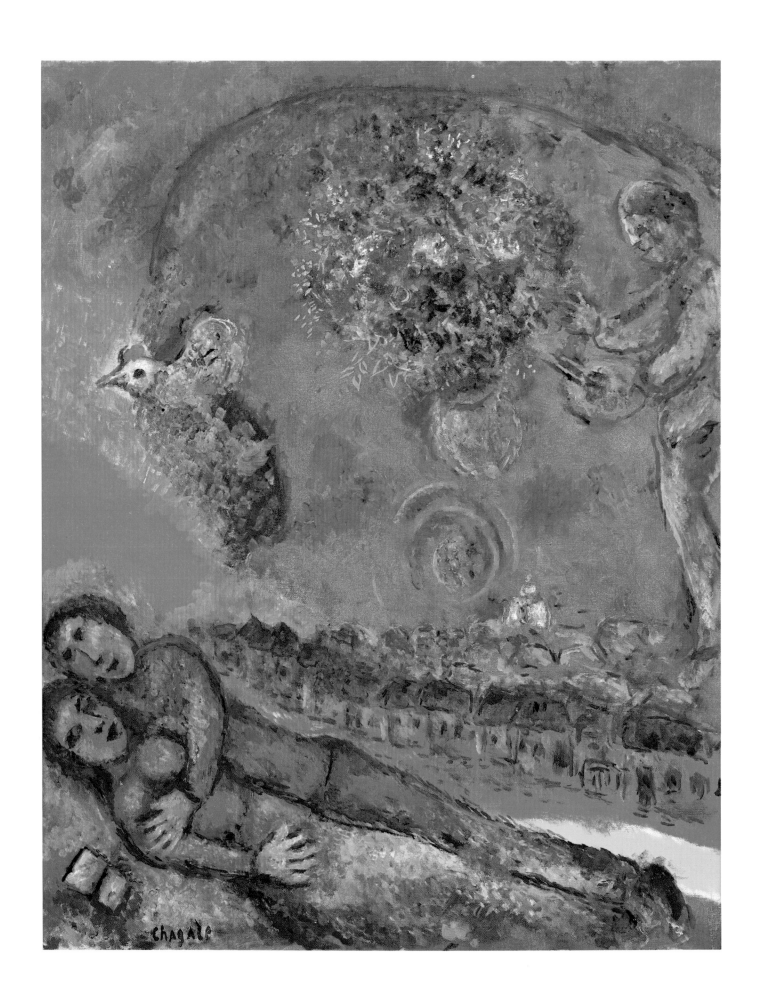

The Late Work
1948–1985

After his return to France, Chagall's work still remained a poetic metaphor for his turbulent life history, a balancing act negotiating dream and reality, an adventure of the imagination that made the invisible visible and thus real. His late work, however, seemed gradually to achieve distance from the twin starting-points in his artistic life, namely, the orthodox Jewish tradition and Russian folklore.

His subject matter, which was taken from his cultural knowledge of a small Russian village, was superseded by the use of motifs from Greek mythology, Christian belief and his own everyday experience. Thus his choice of subjects underwent a cautious change and furthermore the content of his repeatedly deployed symbols was worn away in the course of time. And after 1947 Chagall's links to avant-garde art increasingly weakened almost to the point of non-existence, so that his visual terms came to seem a matter of personal preferences developed over the years, rather than a wish to maintain connections with the latest formal tendencies in the art scene.

But it was not only the artistic market place that Chagall avoided. More and more, he liked to withdraw completely into his private life, and the turbulence of his earlier life was now a thing of the past: in 1950 he moved into a house at Saint-Jean-Cap-Ferrat, and two years later married for the second time. His new beloved was a Russian woman, Valentina Brodsky, whom Chagall tenderly nicknamed Vava. This domestic bliss was to be Chagall's touchstone during this period when his art (and the artist himself) were becoming objects of mounting public interest.

Despite his growing fame, his pictures nevertheless remained as intimate and as naively unworldly in his later years as they had been at the outset. 'Couple on a Red Background' (left) was painted as late as 1983. The man, meaning to win over the woman with tenderness, is placing his arm about the woman's breast, gently inclining his head, trying to look her in the eye, while she, still hesitant, is turning away and looking out at us, as if

The Half-moon Couple, 1951/52
Lithograph, 41.5 × 34.3 cm

Couple on a Red Background, 1983
Oil on canvas, 81 × 65.5 cm
Courtesy of the artist's family

Le Quai de Bercy, 1953
Oil on canvas, 65 × 95 cm
Ida Chagall Collection, Basle

"If a symbol should be discovered in a painting of mine, it was not my intention. It is a result I did not seek. It is something that may be found afterwards, and which can be interpreted according to taste."
MARC CHAGALL

we, by looking at the scene, were disturbing the couple's loving tryst.

The red, which veritably glows in the couple, is matched by a cool blue, and in it, at the right-hand margin, we see the painter himself with a palette in his left hand. It appears as if the vase of flowers is slipping from his open arms, just as the book is being dropped by the lovers. The blue oval echoes the shape of the palette and the bunch of flowers and the bird are no more than abstract dabs of paint.

The images in a painting done exactly thirty years previously, one of a Paris series, are strikingly similar (see above): once again the heart of the composition is occupied by a loving couple, once again there is a bird, and the tree to the left is coloured like a bouquet of flowers. However, Chagall is not merely re-using the same motifs decade after decade; a second parallel between the 1953 and 1983 paintings can also be established. If the seemingly abstract shape of the blue area in the later painting is a larger version of the artist's palette, in the earlier painting we can make out a comparable suggestion of an outsize heart. The tip touches the lower margin of the painting; the heart itself is squarely in the centre of the picture. One diagonal runs to the left into the tree, first serving to indicate the river and the side of the heart; a second line crosses the river to the right and, in the upper half of the painting, is rounded into the typical stylized heart-shape. The symbol of love embraces a loving couple.

In his late work, Chagall was frequently able to endow shapes dictated by technical – that is to say, abstract – reasons with pictorial functions. What seems at first glance to be an arrangement of lines and zones determined along compositional principles turns out to be a sign emphasizing the meaning of the picture, such as the heart. In this way Chagall puts behind him the ideas of the Cubists and the visual concepts of Delaunay, who had once influenced him. In earlier days his wish to base a painting wholly on formal principles, to enmesh it in a purely abstract net, so to speak, was at odds with his aim to present identifiable objects.

This new function of form as a vehicle of a painting's content is matched in many works by a newly liberated use of colour. Slightly late in the day, Chagall took to the kind of *tachiste* painting that Jackson Pollock had initiated in 1947 with his first

Bridges over the Seine, 1954
Oil on canvas, 111.5 × 163.5 cm
Kunsthalle, Hamburg

"The habit of ignoring Nature is deeply implanted in our times. This attitude reminds me of people who never look you in the eye; I find them disturbing and always have to look away." MARC CHAGALL

The Roofs, 1956
Lithograph, 55 × 41 cm

Le Champ de Mars, 1954/55
Oil on canvas, 149.5 × 105 cm
Museum Folkwang, Essen

drip paintings. In 'Bridges over the Seine' (p. 79), for instance, the area of blue can no longer be wholly identified with an object in the composition. On the one hand, it fully covers the reclining couple, yet, on the other, it spreads beyond them and becomes a sort of aura about the embracing lovers. In this as in all his other paintings which betray the influence of American abstract expressionism, Chagall's brush-work is far from spontaneous; it simply reinforces the impression of naive innocence which Chagall, ever subtle in his approach, had always called forth in his figures.

The theme of colour grown autonomous is varied in a number of paintings of flowers at this period, such as 'Le Champ de Mars' (p. 81). The floral motifs afford Chagall a welcome opportunity to indulge in masterly craftsmanship: colour values are savoured, tonal qualities painstakingly harmonized and colour contrasts relished in. These floral elements in the paintings are havens of pure painting, as it were, surrounded by work no less delicately painted, but anchored to a greater extent in the representation of the actual.

A good example of Chagall's use of this new autonomy of colour as a kind of first aid for those who view his work is 'The Concert' (p. 82), painted in 1957. A boat with a couple on board is drifting along a river, with a city on the bank to the right and a group of musicians to the left. The lovers' naked bodies are shrouded in a glowing red that extends upwards beyond their heads. Parallel to this band of colour are two other strips of blue that run from the water to the musicians. These bands suggest that the boat is moving from the bottom right to upper left; so this romantic boating trip, under a full moon, proves in fact to be a voyage from the city cloaked in cool blue to a higher sphere peopled by heavenly musicians.

The Eiffel Tower, the Arc de Triomphe, and Notre-Dame show the city to be Paris, the city where Chagall had his atelier before the war at a time when it was still what it was no longer to be in the aftermath: a great art metropolis. Like many fellow artists, Chagall had turned his back on Paris, and the Côte d'Azur had become a little Montparnasse. It was an apt setting for Chagall, and he was not to leave the region; indeed, in 1967 he built a house large enough for his requirements at Saint-Paul-de-Vence. It contained three studios, one for graphic work, one for drawing, and a third for painting and large-scale designs.

Not long before this final move he completed work on 'Exodus' (p. 83). The title alludes to the exodus of the Israelites from Egypt in 1200 B.C., as recounted in the Old Testament. After crossing the Red Sea in miraculous manner, Moses, the leader, was handed down the Ten Commandments. In the painting he is seen standing at bottom right, holding the tablets with the Commandments, which he has just received from the hand of

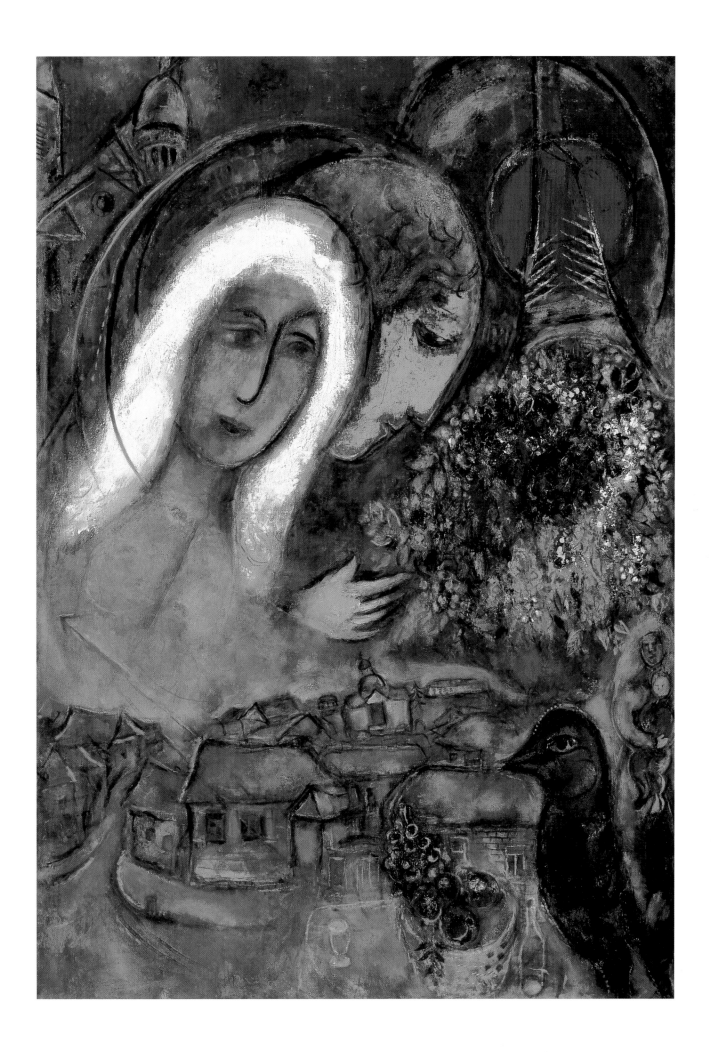

The Concert, 1957
Oil on canvas, 140 × 239.5 cm
Evelyn Sharp Collection, New York

God. Beyond him, a vast crowd is pouring out of the picture's distant depths. These are the people of Israel on the way to their own land, a story which is told as a parable in the Bible and which was also historical reality throughout the Second World War up to the establishment of the State of Israel in 1948. So Chagall sees it – and in the process, in his familiar way, he mixes up the various historical levels and literary sources.

Thoughts of flight and exile re-appear in the painting 'War' (p. 84). A wretched and drastically overloaded cart is slowly putting the burning city behind it. A man is plodding along behind the cart, a sack over his shoulder, saving his worldly goods from the flames. Most of the people here can only just save their lives, though, and cling to each other in confused despair. The people and animals that have remained in the city are helplessly at the mercy of the all-consuming inferno. Chagall feelingly portrays the sufferings people underwent during the war, and by adding to this scenario of cruelty and violence a crucifixion scene in the upper right he elevates the victims of the war to the status of martyrs, who – though themselves guiltless – are forced to bear the burden of expiation.

Modern history paintings of this order were few, and they were not so much reflections of precise historical events as examinations of human suffering; however, Chagall's portraits at this time were even fewer. His two wives were the only people he

honoured with portraits after he quit Russia. In 1966 he painted
Vava (p. 85), his chosen one, seated on a chair, her left arm
resting on the back.

In front of her float a couple of lovers, presumably to remove
any doubts the wife might have had about her husband's affection . . . In the background we see the painter's traditional repertoire of Eiffel Tower, a red animal's head, a village street, but here
they suggest the interior of a studio where Vava, Chagall's muse,
is posing in front of the very paintings she inspired him to create.

"For me, the circus is a magical show, like a world that
comes into being and then is gone again," declared Chagall,
writing of a world that is very closely related to that of his paintings
and which many of his paintings, such as 'The Large Circus' (p.
87) and 'The Grand Parade' (p. 90), pay homage to. Boisterous
merriment and music, a show-case of magic and freakish
oddities, a place where laws have ceased to apply – the descrip-

Exodus, 1952–66
Oil on canvas, 130 × 162 cm
Courtesy of the artist's family

"Changes in societal structure and in art
would possess more credibility if they
had their origins in the soul and spirit. If
people read the words of the prophets
with closer attention, they would find the
keys to life."   MARC CHAGALL

War, 1964–66
Oil on canvas, 163 × 231 cm
Kunsthaus, Zurich

RIGHT:
Portrait of Vava, 1966
Oil on canvas, 92 × 65 cm
Courtesy of the artist's family

tion is as applicable to Chagall's pictures as to the world of the circus. When the painter presents the happy goings-on in the arena, he is expressing in concrete terms the fantasies that otherwise exist only in his dreams, expressing them in terms of a corresponding reality. In the big top, a man who can fly is quite simply a trapeze artiste.

And in 'The Fall of Icarus' (p. 88), the man who so wondrously has wings is not a product of the painter's imagination, but instead derives from Greek myth. Icarus and his father Dedalus built a flying machine to escape from their imprisonment on the island of Crete; but the son, rather too impetuously, flew too close to the sun and the wax that held his wings together melted, so that he lost them and plummeted into the sea. Chagall's painting re-locates the scene of the story, so that the mishap now takes place before the attentive eyes of countless onlookers. The peace of the village is profoundly disturbed by the historic event. While 'The Fall of Icarus' is painted in unusually bright colours to emphasize the special role of the sun in the old tale, in 'The Myth of Orpheus' (p. 89), by contrast, dark shades

84

church of Plateau-d'Assy in Savoy (1957); windows for Metz Cathedral (beginning in 1958); a mural for the foyer of the theatre in Frankfurt (1959); windows for the synagogue of the University Clinic in Jerusalem (1962); windows in the United Nations building in New York, and ceiling paintings in the Paris Opera House (1964); murals in Tokyo and Tel Aviv, and for the Metropolitan Opera in New York (1965); murals for the new parliament building in Jerusalem (1966); mosaics for the University of Nice (1968); stained-glass windows for the Minster of Our Lady in Zurich (1970); mosaics for the Chagall Museum in Nice (1971); windows for Reims Cathedral, and mosaics for the First National

The Large Circus, 1968
Oil on canvas, 170 × 160 cm
Pierre Matisse Gallery, New York

The Fall of Icarus, 1975
Oil on canvas, 213 × 198 cm
Musée National d'Art Moderne,
Centre Georges Pompidou, Paris

The Myth of Orpheus, 1977
Oil on canvas, 97 × 146 cm
Courtesy of the artist's family

Bank in Chicago (1974) and windows for St. Stephen's in Mainz (beginning in 1978).

Neither Chagall nor those who gave him his commissions felt that belonging to a specific religious community need play a decisive part. The artist used his talents equally for synagogues and cathedrals. After all, even the Communist Léger had been allowed to paint a chapel interior! And so had Matisse. When Chagall viewed the decorations Matisse created for the church at Vence, though, he felt that they were unsuited to prayer; his own style was far better for tasks of this nature. It was essential to strike a universal religious note, and the specific images tended to be of secondary significance. The windows he made for the church of All Saints in Tudeley in the county of Kent (England), for example, allude to the death of a girl only incidentally (see p. 91). The girl had drowned in an accident at sea and her parents commissioned the windows and so a private tragedy was heightened, in Chagall's work, by the use of his usual figures and religious symbols. What most engages the eye, however, are motifs taken from Nature, and they, together with the blue that floods everything, achieve the desired mystical mood that prompts us to contemplation and penitence.

"We all know that a good person can be a bad artist. But no one will ever be a genuine artist unless he is a great human being and thus also a good one."
MARC CHAGALL

The Grand Parade, 1979/80
Oil on canvas, 119 × 132 cm
Pierre Matisse Gallery, New York

RIGHT:
St. John, 1978
Stained-glass window, 157.5 × 40 cm
All Saints Church, Tudeley (Kent)

St. Mark and St. Matthew, 1978
Stained-glass window, 131.5 × 34.5 cm
All Saints Church, Tudeley (Kent)

No other twentieth century artist had Chagall's gift for harmonizing what were thought to be irreconcilable opposites. He bridged gaps that had been widening for centuries between different religious communities, ideologies, and not least artistic ideologies. It was this power to integrate that enabled him to satisfy the public's longing for one peaceful family of humanity, one world of brotherly peace. The soothing message was no less than arcadia, paradise and elysium in one. And Marc Chagall, forever travelling between different worlds, was the messenger.

Marc Chagall 1887 - 1985:
A Chronology

1887   Marc Chagall is born in Vitebsk (White Russia) on 7th July, the oldest of nine children, of Jewish parents. His mother, Feige-Ita, is a simple woman. His father, Sachar, works in a herring depot.

1906   Finishes school and attends painter Yehuda Pen's studio as his pupil.

1907   With his friend Mekler he goes to St. Petersburg and studies at the Imperial Society for the Promotion of the Arts.

1908   Changes to the (Svanseva) School, run by Léon Bakst, and remains there until 1910.

1909   Repeated visits to Vitebsk, where he gets to know Bella Rosenfeld, daughter of a jeweller and later to be his wife.

1910   Goes to Paris with funds given by a patron. Fascinated by the intense use of colour in the work of Van Gogh and the Fauves. 'Birth' (p. 11).

1911   Exhibits 'I and the Village' (p. 21) at the Salon des Indépendants. Moves into a studio at 'La Ruche', where Léger, Modigliani and Soutine also live. Friendship with Léger, Cendrars, Apollinaire and Delaunay.

1912   Exhibits at the Salon des Indépendants and the autumn salon. 'The Cattle Dealer' (p. 31).

1913   Through Apollinaire he becomes acquainted with the Berlin art dealer Herwarth Walden and exhibits in an autumn show in Berlin.

1914   First solo exhibition, at Walden's Berlin gallery ('Der Sturm'). Travels from Berlin to Vitebsk, where he is surprised by the outbreak of the First World War. Almost all the works left behind in Paris and Berlin are lost. In St. Petersburg he does war work.

1915   On 25th July he marries Bella Rosenfeld in Vitebsk. In the autumn he moves to Petrograd. 'The Poet Reclining' (p. 40) and 'The Birthday' (p. 38).

1916   Birth of daughter, Ida. Exhibitions in Moscow and Petrograd.

1917/18   Chagall is made Fine Arts Commissar for the Vitebsk region, to which he returns. There he founds a modern school of art, where Lissitzky and Malevich also teach. He arranges celebrations for the first anniversary of the Octo-

The Chagall family in Vitebsk (Marc is standing second from right).

Chagall in 1925.

Chagall (seated, third from left) with the committee of the Vitebsk academy. El Lissitzky is on the far left. Third from right is Yehuda Pen, Chagall's first teacher in Vitebsk. Summer 1919.

Chagall working on the design for a mural for the Jewish Theatre in Moscow. Circa 1920/21.

ber Revolution. The first monograph on Chagall is published. After a quarrel with Malevich he quits the academy. 'Cemetery Gates' (p. 45).

1919/20 Exhibits in the first official show of revolutionary art in Petrograd; the government buys twelve of his paintings. Moves to Moscow and designs murals and decorations for the Jewish Theatre.

1921 Works as a drawing instructor at the Malachovka home for war orphans near Moscow.

1922 Leaves Russia for good and travels to Paris, his wife and daughter following. Legal case concerning 150 of the works left behind in Berlin, which have been sold. Series of etchings entitled 'My Life' done for Cassirer, the art dealer.

1923 Makes his home in Paris. Illustrates Gogol's *Dead Souls* for the publisher Vollard (not published until 1948).

1924 First retrospective in Paris. Summer vacation in Brittany.

1925 Illustrations for La Fontaine's *Fables,* commissioned by Vollard (but not published until 1952). 'Peasant Life' (p. 53).

1926/27 First solo exhibition in New York. Does 19 gouaches for a circus portfolio. Summer in the Auvergne.

1928 Works on the *Fables.* Summer in Céret, winter in Savoy.

Chagall with his palette, 1925.

Chagall giving art classes at the Malachovka home for war orphans near Moscow in 1920.

With Bella, before leaving for Paris, 1922.

1930   Commissioned to illustrate the Bible for Vollard. 'The Acrobat' (p. 59).

1931   His autobiography, *My Life,* is published in Bella's translation. Together with his family he travels to the opening of the museum in Tel Aviv, and studies biblical landscapes in Palestine, Syria and Egypt.

1932   Travels to Holland. Sees Rembrandt's etchings for the first time.

1933   Large retrospective show in the Basle Kunsthalle.

1934/35   Travels to Spain. Impressed by El Greco. Travels to Vilna and Warsaw, and senses the dangers that threaten the Jews.

1937   Becomes a French citizen. A number of his paintings are included in the Nazi exhibition of *Entartete Kunst* (= decadent art) and 59 are confiscated. Travels to Florence. 'The Revolution' (p. 61).

1938   His paintings of the crucifixion recall the sufferings of his people. Exhibits in Brussels. 'White Crucifixion' (p. 63).

1939/40   Receives the Carnegie Painting Prize. When the War breaks out he moves to the Loire, taking his paintings with him, and later to Gordes, in unoccupied Provence.

1941   Travels to Marseille, and from there to New York at the invitation of the Museum of Modern Art, where he arrives on 23rd June, the day the Germans invade Russia.

1942   Spends summer in Mexico, designing the set for Massine's Tchaikovsky ballet *Aleko* for the New York Metropolitan Opera.

Self-portrait, laughing, ca. 1924/25. Etching and cold needle, 27.7 × 21.7 cm. Private collection.

1943   Summer at Cranberry Lake near New York. Chagall is deeply moved by the course of the war in Europe. 'L'Obsession' (pp. 66/67).

1944   Bella dies of a viral infection on 2nd September. For months, Chagall is unable to work. 'The House with the Green Eye' (p. 72).

1945   Resumes painting for the first time since the death of Bella. Designs Stravinsky's ballet-suite *The Firebird* for the Metropolitan Opera.

Chagall in 1930.

1946   Retrospective at the Museum of Modern Art and then in Chicago. First post-war trip to Paris. Coloured lithographs for *The Arabian Nights.*

1947   Exhibition at the Musée National d'Art Moderne in Paris and then in Amsterdam and London. 'Madonna with the Sleigh' (p. 75).

1948   Final return to Paris in August. Lives in Orgeval near Saint-Germain-en-Laye. Wins the first Prize for Graphic Art at the 25th Biennale in Venice.

1949   Moves to Saint-Jean-Cap-Ferrat on the Côte d'Azur. Murals for the Watergate Theatre in London.

1950   Settles in Vence. First ceramic works. Retrospectives in Zurich and Berne.

1951   Travels to Jerusalem for the opening of an exhibition. First sculptures.

1952   On 12th July he marries Juli Valentina (Vava) Brodsky. The publisher Tériade commissions lithographs for 'Daphnis and Chloe'. La Fontaine's *Fables* are published. First visit to Greece with Vava.

1953   Exhibition in Turin. Series of Paris paintings. 'Le Quai de Bercy' (p. 78), 'Bridges over the Seine' (p. 79).

1954   Second trip to Greece. Works on 'Daphnis and Chloe'.

1955/56   Exhibitions in Hanover, Basle and Berne. 'Circus' series of lithographs.

1957   Travels to Haifa for the opening of the Chagall House. Tériade publishes the Bible with his illustrations.

Chagall with his wife Bella and daughter Ida, at work in his Paris studio. 'The Birthday' is behind him. 1927.

In his studio.

Walking in the park in Vence.

Chagall with his second wife, Vava.

1958   Designs the Ravel ballet *Daphnis and Chloe* for the Paris opera. Lectures in Chicago and Brussels. Designs stained-glass windows for Metz cathedral.

1959   Honorary member of the American Academy of Arts and Letters. Honorary doctorate from the University of Glasgow. Exhibitions in Paris, Munich and Hamburg. Mural for the theatre in Frankfurt.

1960   Together with Kokoshka he receives the Erasmus Prize in Copenhagen. Windows for the synagogue of the Hadassah University clinic in Jerusalem.

1962   Travels to Jerusalem for the consecration of the windows. Completes the Metz cathedral windows. Is given the freedom of Vence.

1963   Retrospectives in Tokyo and Kyoto. Travels to Washington.

1964   Travels to New York. Glass windows for the United Nations building. Completes paintings for the ceiling of the Paris opera house.

1965   Murals in Tokyo and Tel Aviv. Starts on paintings for the new Metropolitan Opera and the Lincoln Center in New York, and designs for *The Magic Flute*. Is made an officer of the Legion of Honour.

1966   Mosaics and twelve wall panels for the new parliament building in Jerusalem. Travels to New York for the unveiling of his work for the Lincoln Center. Moves from Vence to his newly-built

house at nearby Saint-Paul-de-Vence. Completes 'Exodus' (p. 83) and 'War' (p. 84).

1967   Attends the production of Mozart's *Magic Flute* on the opening night in New York. Retrospectives to mark his 80th birthday in Zurich and Cologne. Designs three large-scale tapestries for the parliament building in Jerusalem.

1968   Travels to Washington. Glass windows for Metz cathedral. Mosaic for the University of Nice.

1969   Lays the foundation stone of the Message Biblique Institute in Nice. Travels to Israel for the unveiling of his tapestries in the parliament building.

1970   His stained-glass windows for the Zurich minster are consecrated. 'Homage à Chagall' exhibition in the Grand Palais, Paris.

In a café in Saint-Paul-de-Vence.

1972   Begins work on a mosaic for the First National Bank, Chicago.

1973   Travels to Moscow and Leningrad. The Musée National Message Biblique Marc Chagall is opened in Nice.

1974   His windows for Reims cathedral are consecrated. He travels to Russia, and to Chicago for the unveiling of his mosaic.

1975/76   Exhibition of works done on paper in Chicago. Travelling show in five Japanese cities. 'The Fall of Icarus' (p. 88).

1977/78   The French president confers on Chagall the Grand Cross of the Legion of Honour. Visits Italy and Israel. Starts work on windows for St. Stephen's in Mainz. Exhibition in Florence.

1979/80   Exhibitions in New York and Geneva. 'The Psalms of David' in Musée National Message Biblique in Nice.

1981/82   Exhibition of his graphic works in Hanover, Paris and Zurich. Retrospective in the Moderna Museet in Stockholm and the Louisiana Museum in Humlebæk, Denmark (till March 1983).

1984   Retrospectives in the Centre Pompidou in Paris, and in Nice, Saint-Paul-de-Vence, Rome and Basle.

1985   Retrospective at the Royal Academy of Art in London and at the Philadelphia Museum of Art. On 28th March, Chagall dies at Saint-Paul-de-Vence. Retrospective shows of his works done on paper in Hanover, Chicago and Zurich.

The publishers and author would like to thank the museums, collectors, photographers and archives who gave permission to reproduce material. Special thanks are due to the Royal Academy and the publishing house of Weidenfeld & Nicolson, London, for their support. Picture credits: André Held, Ecublens. Archiv Alexander Koch, Munich. Ingo F. Walther, Alling. Quotations from Chagall are taken from his autobiography *My Life* or from Franz Meyer's study of Chagall (DuMont Verlag, Cologne); translations are original to the present publication.

In this series:

- Arcimboldo
- Bosch
- Botticelli
- Bruegel
- Cézanne
- Chagall
- Christo
- Dalí
- Degas
- Delaunay
- Duchamp
- Ernst
- Gauguin
- van Gogh
- Grosz
- Hopper
- Kahlo
- Kandinsky
- Klee
- Klein
- Klimt
- Lempicka
- Lichtenstein
- Macke
- Magritte
- Marc
- Matisse
- Miró
- Monet
- Mondrian
- Munch
- O'Keeffe
- Picasso
- Redon
- Rembrandt
- Renoir
- Rousseau
- Schiele
- von Stuck
- Toulouse-Lautrec
- Turner
- Vermeer
- Warhol